Raising Small Animals for Fun and Profit

Raising Small Animals for Fun and Profit

PAUL VILLIARD

WINCHESTER PRESS

For William

LIBRARY OF CONGRESS CATALOG CARD NUMBER: 72- 79 36 8
ISBN 0-87691-084-3

PUBLISHED BY WINCHESTER PRESS
460 PARK AVENUE, NEW YORK 10022

DESIGNED BY VISUALITY
PRINTED IN THE UNITED STATES OF AMERICA

Acknowledgments

I wish to express my thanks to the staff of Ward's Natural Science Establishment in Rochester, New York, and particularly to Gustav Garay, for their help in supplying material and information.

I am indebted to Mr. Fred Space, of Space Farms, Inc., Beemerville, New Jersey, for allowing me to photograph many animals and for information on mink farming and other phases of small animal management.

The staff of Blue Spruce Farms in Altamont, New York, were also most generous, supplying photographs of raising rats and mice, information, and personal encouragement.

Finally, I thank the many naturalists, teachers, and conservationists who contributed time and knowledge; I appreciate their unselfish efforts.

Contents

Introduction

Millions of small creatures are raised each year for their meat, fur or other products, for sale as pets, for bait and other sporting uses, and for use in laboratories, hospitals, schools, and colleges. They are also raised just for fun. Under the label "fun" come several different reasons for taking the time and trouble to care for and propagate these creatures. Perhaps you want to make a photographic life-history record of a certain animal. Perhaps you want to compile a study collection. Or perhaps you just enjoy observing the behavior and activities of small animals.

Whatever the reason, and, whether you are raising animals as a business or simply as a hobby, certain conditions must be met if you expect any success in your venture. It is my intention to explain these conditions and instruct you in the complexities of rearing small animals, from creatures so small they cannot be seen with the unaided eye, up to animals as large as a raccoon.

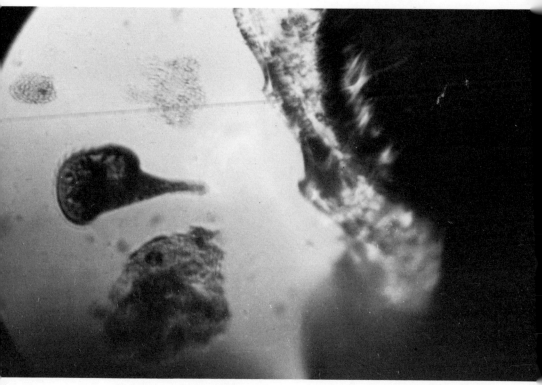

You can start an animal-raising business in a few square feet, if the animals are microscopic, such as *Stentor,* shown here in a photomicrograph.

One of the good things about raising small animals is that you can go into it in as small or as large a way as you desire. You can start with one or two aquariums in your den or basement, raising microscopic organisms, and this can become your entire business. Or you can devote several acres to pens and runs and animal cages, and become a wholesale breeder. The only limit on the size of your venture is the amount of time, effort, and money you wish to spend.

Particularly if you hope to make a business out of raising animals, you should devote some time and thought to just what you want to do and how large an effort you want to undertake, and then prepare yourself before you start with

10

all the information you can gather. Many species of animals are in such constant demand that raising them can be a very profitable venture. Others have a very limited economic use, and unless you have a special market for them there is no point in raising them except as a hobby.

You certainly should not acquire your stock, and *then* try to find out how to keep them and what to do with them. If you don't know how to keep them you will end up with dead stock long before you find out. Each different species of animal requires a different type of ecosystem—some of them very simple, some of them complicated. Whichever the type, you must provide it, or you will have nothing but failure and a loss of your creatures.

One business that has sprung up only within the last few years is raising game birds. It is a lot of work, but evidently the returns justify the expenditure of time and effort, and it is a good example of a sound commercial venture. The Chinese ring-necked pheasant is the most commonly reared bird, and other game birds are now being added to the list. A land owner with a large tract of wooded land will often list his land as a shooting range and charge a hunting fee by the day, hour, week, or even the entire season. Usually the landowner will guarantee a catch, and the game sought is the pheasant and partridge. So he will buy birds from a professional breeder and release hundreds or even thousands of them on the preserve to serve as targets for the nimrods out after sport.

It is true that raising game birds, like most other small-animal ventures, is possible only in rural areas. But by the same token, such ventures may make it possible to live in an area where employment is scarce. Many city dwellers would very much like to live in the country or a rural district, but do not have the courage to move, because of the possibility of being unable to make a living. If you are in this position, you might hedge your bet by purchasing acreage close enough to the city in which you work so that if necessary you could commute to an office each day. There is, of course, the inconvenience of commuting, but this inconvenience is far outweighed by the pleasure and restfulness of country living and the possibility of finding local sources of income.

The raising of small animals has made it possible for many people to give up their city apartments in exchange for a comfortable place in the quiet rural areas. So it was in my own case. When the pressures of city living became so intense that I thought I would not be able to survive another month, I bought just three acres of country land, put up a very small one-room cabin, and moved there to rear moths—of all creatures. My three acres soon became a butterfly farm, and I was deeply involved with these fragile and lovely creatures. I found a ready market for the cocoons among breeders and collectors all over the world. I joined an entomological society in order to find other people interested in the same business.

We now have a very large house on the original land, but no longer a butterfly farm. I have turned to other adventures, but still enjoy the peace and restful quiet of my country home. Of course, I still am called "that worm fellow" by some of the people in town, who think it was a little peculiar of me, having bought woods land, to cut down most of the trees only to plant different trees, then cage the new growth and put "worms" inside the cages to eat up all the fresh leaves.

I still get mail from people who have read works of mine and want to buy stock to begin rearing for themselves. I still, every now and then, receive a letter from some university or laboratory, asking if I could supply cocoons of some large moth or other, in lots of 10,000, for which they have a government grant. So if I wished I could still earn my living as a moth farmer.

Small animals can help the rural dweller in other ways too. Meat, one of the biggest items on the budget these days, can be augmented by raising rabbits for food. This is an ideal occupation for children, since rabbits are less difficult to care for than other animals. Rabbit meat is a delicacy coming more and more into favor in the United

States, and rabbits have long been a staple source of meat in European countries. The only danger in having youngsters raise rabbits for meat is that they may make pets out of them, then dissolve in grief when they are killed for food. They should start out with the understanding that the ultimate aim is to stock the freezer with succulent meat. They can, if they like, segregate one or two animals for their own pets, these being the breeding stock, destined to live out their lives rather than end up in the pot.

Surplus rabbits find a ready sale as meat animals or as pet animals among rural neighbors. The local pet stores can also take some for resale. Also the hides have a market; the yellow pages of a rural phone book should list dealers in leather and hides who are all prospective purchasers of rabbit hides. The fur dealers—wholesale dealers, that is—will purchase skins of mink and other precious fur animals, and also rabbit hides with good fur for use in making garments.

If you want to get into the big time with rabbits, the magazine *Rabbit World* would be your trade journal. It lists advertisements of persons who wish to buy rabbits live, dressed for meat, the hides, and fur. The large felt companies throughout the country are sources of sale for the hair of angora rabbits, which is used in making fine felt. If you try several of these companies, you should be able to make a contract to sell all the fur you can deliver. Bear in mind, however, that these companies are not interested in purchasing the fur from one or two rabbits. They need fur in large quantities, and unless you want to go in for rearing a herd large enough to make a good quantity of fur, you should not bother trying to market the product.

Tanning companies are another good source of sale for the pelts, and country butcher shops for dressed rabbits, or even for killed rabbits unskinned. They will often do their own skinning.

In some regions of this country commercial rabbit growers and meat slaughterhouses buy rabbits in quantity from small breeders. These firms usually maintain a truck pickup service, making regular route stops at the small producer's rabbitry. Your local chamber of commerce should be able to tell you if there is such a market within a reasonable distance of your place.

Rabbits, as well as guinea pigs, hamsters, rats, and mice, are sold to laboratories, often in fairly large quantities. Laboratory supply houses and biological supply houses are also good prospects for sale of these animals. All of the large chemical laboratories buy small animals in quantity. Lederle Laboratories Division of American Cyanamid Company, Pearl River, New York, 10965; Sharpe and Dohme Laboratories, Glenolden, Pennsylvania, 19036; the National Institute of Health, Rockville Pike, Bethesda, Maryland, 20014, are three such places where you can sell your products.

But if you do not live in the country now and are unwilling to risk a move, there are still animals discussed in this book that you can raise for a profit. Protozoa can be sold to schools during the school year. You should contact your local school board for the names of the purchasing agents, and also the individual science teachers at the school, who often are permitted to make their own purchases, especially in high schools and higher grades. Every university and college buys protozoa for study work. (Science teachers also often purchase mice and rats for their biology classes, and buy baby chicks for genetics study.) If you deliver quality goods, promptly, you should be able to get individual teachers to buy from you on a regular basis, whatever quantity they use each year, and thus work up a regular sales schedule that will enable you to run the business in an orderly manner.

Tropical fish are also suitable for an urban business, though they are more difficult to sell. They have a ready sale in quantities of from 25 to 100 to pet shops, but other than that they must be sold on an individual retail basis. Some years ago I started in the tropical-fish business and met with some success. True, at that time the hobby was in its starting years, and 90 percent of the fish sold were wild imports, taken from jungle streams and flown into this country at some expense and trouble. Prices were high. Today, fish that I sold at $15 a pair—and I was unable to meet the demand even at that price—might sell for $1.29 a pair. I was able to sell *Symphysodon discus* for $500 a pair at breeding size; today you can get the same fish for around $15 each.

This is because in the intervening years, people have learned to breed these rare fishes in aquariums in their own homes, and the supply is now nearly inexhaustible. This is why, in the chapter on tropical fish, I advise you to specialize in one or maybe two of the rarer kinds of fish, and to investigate the market before you attempt to breed them for sale. Usually the same kinds of fishes are popular all over the country, but your local pet stores may have a preference of one kind or other, and this is the one you should try.

Of course, not every business involving small animals is a sound one, and it is possible to lose money in this kind of venture as in any other. You must calculate your risks and your chances of success. For example, if you want to start a retail tropical-fish business, you should first determine, by actual investigation, how far away the nearest existing shop is. If it is rather close to you, then unless you live in New York, Chicago, San Francisco, or another large city where there are enough people to absorb several similar businesses, it is better not to start, since you will be unable to meet the immediate competition of the established business.

And consider your investment. You would have to determine to sink anywhere from $5,000 to $10,000 in a fish store to begin, and it will take you from three to five years to get back your money. Also, the losses are high when you first start out. The water in your locality must be experimented with in order to learn how to best condition it for the fishes you intend to keep. You must have a source of purchase of stock for sale, since you could not possibly hope to rear all your selling stock yourself—you would be in a full-time breeding business with no time off to take care of customers

Baby raccoons are endearing, and the beginning small animal raiser might think they were ideal to raise for sale as pets—but in fact the market for them is very small, and they become rough and even dangerous when mature. They are an example of an animal that should be raised only for fun, not for profit.

16

if you tried. There are several wholesale fish companies in the country, most of them in New York City, San Francisco, and in Florida. But the fish are shipped by air, and the losses are fairly high.

From experience, I would strongly suggest that you limit yourself to breeding a popular kind of fish and selling the young to pet stores. You can, with a minimum of trouble, solicit business from stores within a radius of, say, 100 or 150 miles. This trip is not too long for you to take once a month or every two months to deliver your stock to the shops. Within that radius you should find several pet stores, each of which would be able to take a fair number of sound, healthy fish at regular intervals. Again, if you are dependable, sell only prime stock, and deliver when you promise, you should have no trouble working up' regular customers who are willing to take your entire output. Remember, though, that young fishes bring only a few cents each, and you have to sell large numbers to make it pay.

In this volume I will explain how to raise many kinds of small animals, for whatever the reason you choose. What you do with them is up to you, though I will give you some suggestions. Certain animals are protected by state laws, or even by federal laws. You should carefully investigate laws governing the particular species you decide to raise before attempting to obtain your stock—there may be regulations you must meet before going into the business. Most game birds and many other small animals such as raccoons, mink, and fox are regulated in some way. A letter to the department of conservation at your state capital will bring you free information on all species. An appendix of the addresses for each state is in the back of this book.

PAUL VILLIARD
Saugerties, N.Y.
1972

PART I

MICROZOOLOGY

CHAPTER I

Equipment Used for Microzoology

When you raise rabbits or any other common small animal, you must have the proper equipment—cages of the correct kind, feeding dishes, watering devices, and so on. It is just the same with microscopic animals, though the equipment is somewhat different. The most complicated and expensive item of equipment for this work is a microscope. You must have some kind of magnifying device, because the animals you are raising are so small that they cannot be seen with the unaided eye.

A good compound microscope with two or three lenses is a very costly item. You san spend from $125 for a rather inferior scope to $800 or even $1,000 for a really good one with all the elaborate attachments for photography, dark field illumination, and other refinements.

But be of good cheer. You do not need a laboratory-quality microscope, at least to start with. Fortunately there is a way to avoid this enormous outlay of money. The Bausch and Lomb Optical Company makes classroom microscopes with inexpensive plastic parts but really good lenses. They are made in single powers—10X, 40X, 100X—and cost just a few dollars. These are ideal for examining microscopic animals, and I would certainly suggest all three as a set, since some of your animals will require higher magnification than others. If you do not get all three at the beginning, then I would settle for the 10X and the 100X. However, you will shortly find the middle one useful as well.

These microscopes do not have eyepieces designed for cameras, but, with a little ingenuity, one can fit a camera to them and get some very creditable photographs. Since the lenses are very good, the images obtained with these school scopes are better than average. Bausch and Lomb also makes a little light to use with the instruments.

There are also available several small microscopes made in Japan, some of which might prove useful in your work.

Binocular microscopes are excellent for examination of tiny animals, but they are quite expensive. Of course, if you are going into rearing protozoans for profit instead of for fun, investing in certain expensive pieces of equipment may be quite justifiable.

You will need a supply of culture dishes. These are sold by the dozen or by the case, and most biological supply companies stock them. The standard culture dish—sometimes called a syracuse dish—is about 4 inches in diameter and 1½ inches deep. The dish has a lip on the bottom to permit stacking, and in use, anywhere from six to a dozen dishes are stacked as they are filled with the culture medium and animals, remaining stacked as the cultures propagate. It is from these dishes that the cultures are divided and sold.

Pipettes, eye droppers, tweezers, inoculating needles, and loupes are all useful and needed in rearing protozoa. All these are to be found in any biological supply house, and none of them is very expensive. As you get deeper into rearing the tiny creatures, you will find other items useful, and these can be obtained as they are needed. Microscope slides for examination of your cultures, immobilizing medium for tranquilizing the animals for study, and other aids then be put through the freezing and refrigeration schedule as for crickets: freezing for two or three days, and refrigeration for about a month.

Water must be supplied to the young nymphs, but like young crickets they are likely to drown in a drinking dish. A small bottle or test tube, stoppered with a tight twist of cotton or a dental roll and placed on a slant so the water touches the inside end of the plug, will serve very well. The insects can take their moisture as it percolates through the dental roll or the cotton. Check the water supply often, making sure the wick is in contact with the water and adjusting the slant of the bottle if necessary. Dental rolls can be purchased at dental supply houses, or your own dentist might supply you with a few.

Grasshoppers require sunlight and warm temperatures. They also require well-ventilated cages. If you are using the large ashcans, you should cut holes an inch in diameter in each can near the bottom and cover them with squares of screening, fastening the screening with either tape or epoxy glue. These holes will create a chimney effect and cause a constant circulation of air up through the can. If you use copper screening instead of plastic or aluminum, you can solder it to the can. (Galvanized screening can also be soldered, but it is apt to rust in a comparatively short time.) Make certain, of course, that there are no gaps around the edges of the screens, because the grasshoppers, especially young ones, can squeeze out between the screen and the can if the screening is not tightly in place.

Another excellent kind of cage can be made of screening all around, except at the bottom. Such a cage allows complete circulation of air, the clear admission of sunlight, and places for the insects to cling, permitting a greater population density than when only the floor area is available for living space. A screen cage should be made with a tightly fitted door for easy access. The bottom should be removable if possible. Such cages are sold for the purpose, or you can make them if you are handy with tools.

Their diet consists mainly of grasses, grains, fruits, and tubers. In captivity they will take nearly all kinds of vegetables and fruits, and the clippings from lawns, weed leaves like dandelion and plaintain, lettuce, cabbage leaves, and similar substances. Unless their diet includes a good amount of fruit having a lot of juice, you will need to keep water dishes in the cages. They should also be sprayed lightly once a day.

The egg containers should be larger and deeper than for crickets. Bread pans do very well, and these should be filled with clean sterile sand, dampened and kept damp. It is best to wash the sand thoroughly, then bake it in the oven for about four hours at 400 degrees before using it. You need not sow the sand with any kind of seed, but you can if you wish, and if you do it may supply succulent young shoots for the adults while they are laying.

Unless you actually observe the females thrusting their ovipositors under the sand, you may not know when eggs are laid. You can check periodically by removing the trays and sifting the sand through a coarse strainer. The grasshoppers eggs will appear as small pods in the sand. If such pods are present, they should be reburied and the tray may

Young grasshoppers, hatched in early summer. By fall they will be 2 inches or more in length.

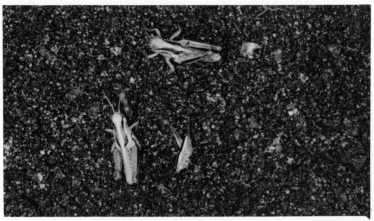

The author examining a culture of protozoa under a binocular zoom microscope. Much less expensive equipment will also suffice.

23

will be helpful as your rearing techniques develop. A small accurate gram scale is required for weighing out the ingredients of the culture mediums, unless you purchase ready-made mediums from the biological suppliers. It is easier to purchase the medium, but cheaper to make your own. A small amount goes a long way—a pint bottle makes up to a dozen cultures.

Many of the microscopic animals that are commonly raised are protozoa. The usual definition of protozoa is that they are simple one-celled animals, and the subject is not carried further. This definition is not exactly correct. It's true that most are unicellular, but the single cell may be of much greater complexity than any cell in your own body. Also, some are technically unicellular, but exist only in colonies of many individuals.

Some animals usually grouped with the protozoa, like the rotifers, are multicellular, even though they are no larger than many unicellular animals and have the same habitats. Finally, some living objects commonly considered protozoa are not even animals but have more in common with plants.

Protozoa and other microscopic creatures belong to a hidden world of wonder, and their daily lives are of intense interest to the student of nature or to the budding scientist. They are also useful as subjects to be raised for various reasons.

There are perhaps more than 20,000 classified species protozoa, and certainly there are many more thousands yet to be classified. A drop of water from almost any pond will abound in these creatures; sometimes a dozen or more different kinds will be found in the same drop. Bear in mind that a drop of water to them is as an ocean to us. As to the typical protozoan being a simple animal, an hour spent in observing a living colony of volvox, for example, will soon dispel that theory. The complexity and beauty of these creatures is astonishing.

Many scientific supply houses sell cultures of various protozoa, and these companies have special laboratories in

Wards' Natural Science Establishment in Rochester, N.Y., cultures protozoa commercially. The protozoa are cultured in small flasks, then stored in stackable dishes; they are measured out into jars for shipment to schools and laboratories.

which they are reared. Sometimes this rearing becomes a very well-run scientific business, and the equipment used is very costly. In order to rear protozoa you need not go into it as extensively as do these companies, but you will have to learn sound laboratory procedures in order to ensure the continuance of your cultures, and, even more importantly, in order to maintain the purity of a strain. Unless you can isolate and rear specimens individually, you will have no market for your product. By individually I do not mean single specimens in isolated tanks, but rather, individual species of protozoa separate from each other.

If you are intending to raise several different kinds of microscopic animals, it will be easier to purchase cultures from one of the large and reputable houses rather than to try to locate and isolate the species from the wild. However, some of them are so easily taken that you may like to hunt for your own in a pond near you. Therefore I explain in subsequent chapters the equipment and technique you need to capture the most common protozoa as well as to raise them.

CHAPTER 2
Hydras

Hydras are not protozoa—they are many-celled polyps, and they are much larger than most protozoa. But since they are visible to the naked eye and are widely distributed in the same waters in which protozoa are found, hunting for them is a good way to begin a career in microzoology.

Hydras are the freshwater relations of a very large group of marine animals, and they have a limited ability of locomotion. It is most interesting to watch a hydra move about by its peculiar somersaulting method of bending down to place the head end on the support, then releasing its "foot," straighten up to repeat the movement, and end by again standing erect nearly two lengths away from where it started. Another method of travel is a kind of gliding motion. This is also readily seen in a relative of the hydra—the anemone. These larger saltwater relations also glide slowly and deliberately, when they wish to move about.

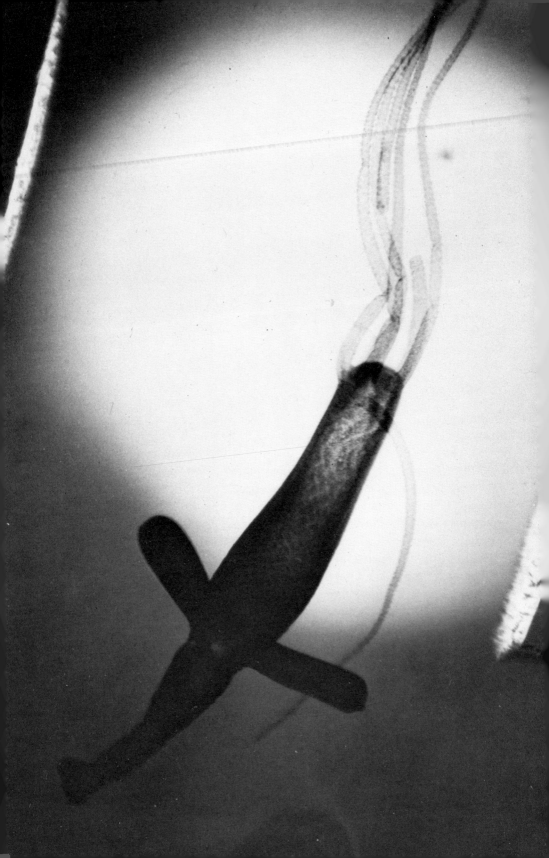

Hydras are carnivorous animals, and require regular feeding of other animals. The "water flea" is one of the easiest foods to obtain for your hydra culture. Water fleas are tiny crustaceans, visible to the naked eye as fast moving specks in clear water, under the low-power microscope they look like transparent fleas or lobsters. They are difficult to rear, but can be purchased from the local pet store if you are unable to find them in the wild. While a water flea is sometimes much larger in diameter than a hydra, still the polyp has no difficulty ingesting its prey.

In construction, a hydra is a short threadlike animal having one or more tiny protuberances on the sides, and a ring of tentacles at the top. In the center of the top, inside the ring of tentacles, is the opening of the mouth. This opening also serves for the emission of waste material in most polyps. The tentacles of hydras are quite complicated. They contain many cells or capsules containing threads bearing a poison apparatus. While these threads are harmless to human beings, they prove deadly enough to the prey of the hydra. When a water flea or other small animal contacts a tentacle, these threads shoot out like coiled springs, stinging the creature and immobilizing it. Other threads wrap around the victim, holding it fast. The tentacles then engulf the prey, drawing it down into the gullet, which stretches to accommodate the size. A hydra has no difficulty swallowing a water flea twice its own diameter. The poison threads are discarded, and new ones grow in their place.

Hydras can be raised in a small aquarium, one with a capacity of about 2 to 5 gallons. If you intend to stock your culture with wild-caught specimens, you should have a 5-gallon bucket—preferably a plastic one. The pails in which building materials such as taping compound are sold make ideal collecting buckets. These pails are usually returned to the building supply houses for a cash refund of 25 cents, and the companies will usually sell them to you either for the same amount, or for a small profit. In any event, they are strong, have good handles, and are far cheaper than a regular plastic pail.

A hydra reproducing asexually—the two buds will eventually break off and live as separate animals.

Along the edges of ponds, where the water is still, is the best location to collect hydras. They are not free-swimming in the water, but attached to dead leaves, twigs, water plants growing under the surface, and floating water plants such as duckweed, salvia, and nitella. Take a quantity of the floating plants, and a good scoop of the bottom detritus, including some of the mud from the bottom, and dump it into the pail. Fill the pail with water from the same area by dipping it out in a smaller container and pouring it into the pail. You will have a bucket full of mucky water when you are finished, but this will settle in your aquarium and become quite clear.

If you notice many free-swimming creatures in the water at the pond, it would be well if you strained the water you dip out through a piece of old sheet or muslin. Some of the free-swimmers may be water fleas, but others probably are predators that will feed on the hydras. There is no need to introduce enemies into your rearing tank. The mud and leaves, twigs, and other detritus you bring along will contain many different species of tiny animals that will serve admirably as food for your hydras.

At home you can pour the mud, leaves, and other material into the tank you are going to use for your hydra culture, and place the tank where it will obtain some daylight and perhaps an hour or two of sunlight each day. Too much sunlight will cause the water to turn green with overgrowths of algae.

If it is impossible to select a location with sufficient light, then you must use artificial lighting. There are several ways to obtain enough light on an aquarium. One is by the use of a regular aquarium hood—made of stainless steel and housing one or more fluorescent tubes. Some hoods have sockets for incandescent bulbs, and if the one you obtain is this type, a 25-watt bulb is plenty strong enough. A regular gooseneck reading lamp is also usable, and this should be bent to point the reflector at the end of the tank. Six to eight hours each day should be sufficient to promote growth in your culture tank. If the water seems to be overloaded with

30

green algae, cut the light down an hour or two until it adjusts itself. If the culture seems to languish, increase the illumination by a couple of hours per day.

After the water has stood a day or two it should clear. Now when you look at the leaves and twigs against the light you should be able to see hydras clinging to them. There may be a great many, or only a few. Sometimes you will get a batch of material with none at all. This should not discourage you. Try a new site, or even try the same site at a different time of the day, or at a time when the temperature is different.

The culture tank should be covered by a sheet of glass, but space must be left to permit the exchange of air over the water surface. This is easily accomplished by taping a narrow strip of thin cardboard to the edge of the glass in one or more places. The glass will rest on the strips, leaving a slight gap through which air can enter.

The water you gathered with the culture should contain enough different organisms to feed your hydras. If, for some reason, the water is nearly barren, then you should introduce a colony of water fleas in order to ensure continuance of the hydra population. Daphnia—one type of water flea— may be purchased from almost any pet store, or cultures can be purchased from biological supply houses. If you are unable to find any wild hydras, a culture of these, too, may be had from the same source.

Hydras are used in schools and in laboratories for experimental purposes, mainly regeneration studies. They have, in common with most of their relatives, the ability to regenerate all or a part of their bodies. If a hydras is dissected in a horizontal plane, the top half will soon grow a new bottom, and the bottom half a new head. The animal may even be cut into segments, and each segment will regenerate into a complete hydra.

Hydras reproduce either sexually or asexually. During most of the year the reproduction is asexual. A small bud forms on the side of the parent hydra, soon growing to nearly full size, when it finally breaks off to live as a complete and separate animal. This will happen at frequent intervals.

In the fall hydras tend to reproduce sexually. This sexual reproduction may be initiated in captivity by dropping the temperature of the tank in which they are grown. When the temperature of the water reaches between 50 and 60 degrees, the hydras will pair off for mating. The eggs are formed in one hydra and the sperm in another. The "male" hydras sheds his sperm into the water, where it is free-swimming. The eggs are fertilized on the female, then drop off to hatch into tiny replicas of the parents.

Hydras thrive best in water that has a neutral acidity-alkalinity balance (pH 7.0), although they will live and even multiply in water as acid as pH 6.0 and as alkaline as nearly pH 9.0. Any adjustments made to the pH of a culture should be done very gradually over a period of several days, rather than all at once. Methods of adjusting pH are described in detail in Chapter 13.

CHAPTER 3
Paramecia

These slipper-shaped animals are familiar to almost everyone who has ever had anything at all to do with school science. They are one of the few protozoa large enough to be seen with the naked eye—provided your naked eye is sharp and clear.

Several interesting things are known about paramecia. One is the rapid and accurate sensing device they possess. The shape of a paramecium is such that a sample of the water ahead of the animal is constantly being fed back to the creature as it swims about. Paramecia are ciliates, which means that they have rows of short hairlike structures on their body that constantly wave, like banks of oars. These tiny hairs are called cilia, and they make currents in which the creatures move. On one side, facing the front end, is a groove, also lined with cilia. This is called the oral groove, and it is through this groove that the animal takes in its food. As the animal swims, the water ahead is moved down into the oral groove. If the water is too acid, too alkaline, too hot, or too cold, the tiny creature immediately backs away, then darts off in a new direction. If, on the other hand, the sample of water is rich in bacteria, which the animal eats, it continues on its path, feeding as it goes.

Almost every pond contains paramecia, sometimes in great abundance. You may collect them as one does hydra—by scooping up muck and leaves from the bottom of the pond near the edges, and also taking some of the surface scum and weeds. You will also need several gallons of the water from the same area, again screening it through a layer of cloth to eliminate the larger predators.

Paramecia are one of the most-used animals in schools. They are used in many experiments. They reproduce both sexually and by division. For the most part, paramecia in a single culture will only divide. The reason for this was not known for a long time, but finally it was realized that there are several strains or types of paramecia, and that only different mating strains are able to reproduce sexually. After this became known, laboratories and biological supply houses began to rear the different strains, keeping them pure. So now, if you wish to rear paramecia sexually, you must specify the different mating strains with which to do so. However, the specimens in each strain, while they will not mate sexually, still will multiply by division, and so will a culture of wild animals you collect from your pond.

If one paramecium were placed in a tank all by itself and permitted to reproduce by division, and if all the progeny survived, the bulk of the animals would exceed the volume of the earth within 115 paramecium generations! But this cannot happen in fact; it is only a statistic.

Feeding paramecia is performed in a kind of left-handed fashion. Actually, you must raise colonies of certain bacteria, and then feed these to the paramecia. Bacteria cultures are not as difficult as they may sound. Here are several ways to start them going.

1. To one quart of water add about 20 grains of rice. Boil the water and rice for 3 or 4 minutes, then pour it into a small tank or other container and let it stand uncovered in a light place, but not in direct sunlight, and at room temperature.

2. To a quart of boiled water placed in a container as before, add a paste made from about ½ teaspoonful of

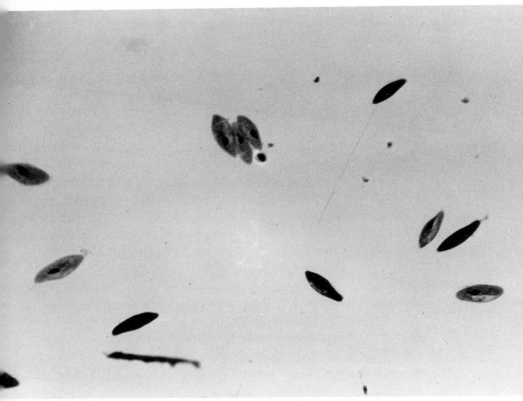

Paramecia under the microscope. One of the larger protozoa, they are just barely visible to the naked eye as minute specks in almost any pond water.

hardboiled egg yolk mixed with a little of the boiled water. The egg should be boiled for about 20 minutes.

3. Take a small handful of timothy hay that has been chopped into short pieces, add it to a quart of water, and boil for 3 or 4 minutes. The entire stew is poured into the container.

Within a couple of days, each of these cultures should have striving colonies of bacteria in them, and the liquid may be poured into the paramecium culture tank, adding the paramecium culture to this preparation. It is well to renew the culture about once a month, by preparing a new infusion of the hay, rice, or egg yolk, placing it in a clean, well-washed container, and then dipping out a few paramecia from the old culture and introducing them to tho new.

In this manner you will always have thriving cultures that will rapidly increase their populations.

In order to manipulate or transfer single specimens of protozoa from one place to another, it is necessary to have some small pipettes. These micropipettes are easily made with a little practice. Soft soda-glass or lime-glass tubing is obtainable from scientific supply houses. A short length of this tube, softened in the flame of a bunsen burner, or even over the gas flame of the kitchen range, then pulled straight apart as soon as the glass is soft enough to give, will result in two pipettes. You may have to snap off the extremely fine hairlike point of each half of the tubing in order to expose the hole in the end.

The pipette may be used in either of two ways. You may close off the large end with a fingertip, stick the other end into the culture, then release the top end to permit the water (and the animals) to be sucked up into the tube. Then close off the end again as you raise the pipette, which will keep the water within it, and release the water into the new container (or onto a microscope slide).

The second method, which is perhaps more convenient until you have practice using a pipette, is to make the pipette out of a short section of glass tubing, then force this into a short section of rubber tubing, only partway. The other end of the rubber tubing is then stopped with a very small rubber cork or a short length of solid glass rod. Now, by squeezing the rubber tube, you may operate the pipette as you would an eye dropper.

Indeed, an eye dropper may be used for some things. It is, however, generally too gross to work with in handling these small creatures, and the pipette will be found infinitely more useful. You can improve an eye dropper by heating it in the middle and then pulling it apart, as described above for making pipettes from glass tubing.

CHAPTER 4
Amoebas

The most primitive animal on earth is the amoeba. It is also one of the most interesting. It is unicellular, amorphous in shape, and keeps changing its shape constantly. The animal has the ability to throw out pseudopods. A pseudopod is a globby extension of part of the body, which extends like a questing foot and comes to rest, and then the entire balance of the body flows back into it, creating the queer flowing movement of the animal.

Amoebas are fashioned of a membrane so thin that it is invisible, even under powerful magnification, filled with jellylike protoplasm. When the animal feeds it merely flows up to its prey or food particle, then engulfs it within itself.

Amoebas are responsible for several diseases of man—among the most notable is dysentery. Not all amoebas cause diseases. Some of them spend their lives in certain other animals, being indigenous only to those species. These parasitic amoebas do not always infect their hosts with a

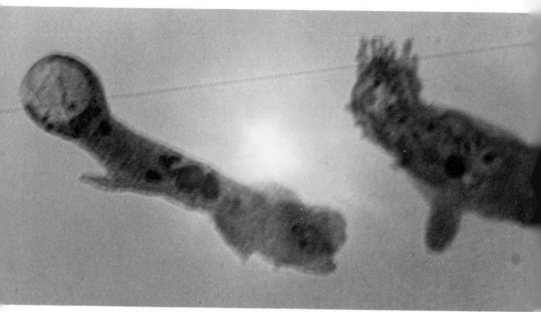

Amoebas are shapeless and almost transparent—the best way to find them under the microscope is to keep the light level very low.

disease, but live quietly in the intestinal tract and cause no harm.

Amoebas have complete regeneration ability. Or, to be more exact, since they actually have no true shape, if a fragment of an amoebra contains a nucleus, it will grow to full size as though nothing had happened to it. It is hard to say that the animal can regenerate when there is no head, foot, tentacle, or other recognizable feature to grow back.

Some amoebas are quite large. About the biggest of them all is *Pelomyxa carolinensis,* a true giant of protozoa. This animal may reach a length of 3 millimeters or more—plenty large enough to be seen easily without the aid of magnification. The species most reared in laboratories is *Amoeba proteus.* This one, and other species, can be purchased in pure cultures from biological supply houses, and thereafter you can maintain your own cultures. Since *Pelomyxa* amoebas are multinuclear, one of them may be separated into many fragments and each fragment that contains a nucleus will grow to full size.

Amoebas are rather difficult to find in the wild, and therefore it is better to depend on a purchased culture to start. If you want to try your hand at amoeba hunting, look in ponds with growths of reeds and cattails and floating plants such as waterlilies and lotus. You may find the little creatures clinging to the undersides of the leaves, and around the stems of the reeds that are under water.

Amoebas should be observed under dim lighting, since they are so transparent that under intense light they tend to be invisible. Crosslighting is an even better way to view them. Once located, it is easy to isolate each individual specimen in order to transfer it to a culture tank. Here, because of their size, you would use an eyedropper instead of a pipette, sucking up the amoeba and squirting it into the prepared culture bath.

A peculiar thing about purchasing amoeba cultures is that you are more than likely, upon arrival of the container, to find it full of tiny fragments of the animals, none of them intact or full size. They have a tendency to fragment during the rough handling through the mail. No matter. If you dump them into their rearing tank, you will soon find each fragment that contains a nucleus growing into a perfect amoeba in a few days.

If you are rearing the creature for sale to school or laboratories, it is wise to inform your prospective customers of this possibility, or they may complain that they are receiving damaged goods.

Feeding your culture of amoebas requires much the same procedures as feeding paramecia. That is, both paramecia and amoebas feed on bacteria, which can be generated in hay, rice, or egg-yolk solutions.

Cultures of amoebas are in great demand among laboratories specializing in the study of parasitology. Universities usually have departments devoted to this study, and they purchase amoeba cultures beside rearing their own strains.

CHAPTER 5
Volvox

Of all the protozoa, and, truly, of nearly all living animals, I think the volvox is the most beautiful. It is one of the protozoa that are neither plant nor animal. It is assigned to the algaes. Actually each globe of volvox is a colony of from 125 to 10,000 individual cells. Each cell is connected to the adjoining one by strands of cytoplasm, and each cell contains a nucleus, a chloroplast, a stigma, and two flagella. The cells are arranged in the outer wall of a hollow sphere in such a way that the flagella are on the outside of the sphere. Consequently the whole colony is like a bristly ball. Actually, the flagella are so fine that they cannot be seen except under high magnification. The colonies of volvox themselves, however, can be watched quite comfortably under a 20X glass.

It is truly wonderful to watch a culture of volvox majestically swimming in the water. They move with grace and deliberation, constantly revolving as they travel about. You can look right through each colony with no difficulty. Some of the colonies contain even smaller spheres. These are filial colonies caused by reproduction.

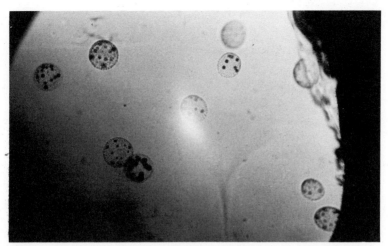
Volvox. Each sphere consists of many individual cells, and the smaller contained spheres are daughter colonies that will eventually be released from the parent colonies.

Volvox reproduce both asexually and sexually. In asexual reproduction some of the cells in a colony enlarge to form the filial colonies, which are held within the parent sphere. When they reach a certain growth, they are released through a rent in the outer wall of the main colony. This method of reproduction is carried on throughout the year. In the fall, volvox begin to reproduce sexually. Instead of forming filial colonies, they make zygotes. In the parent colony are two sizes of cells—microgametes and macrogametes. The latter are by far the larger. A pair of these unequal cells unite to form a zygote, which falls to the bottom ooze in the pond and there overwinters. In the spring, the zygote grows into a new colony, which repeats the cycle of asexual reproduction once more.

Volvox cultures are grown in soil-water medium. This is merely a good garden soil with some humus content, mixed with distilled water. The water should be steamed for an hour or so before using. Special volvox medium is available from biological supply houses if you do not want to make your own.

PART II

INSECTS

CHAPTER 6
Crickets

As insects go, crickets are quite large; some species are several inches long. However, we are not concerned with these species as much as we are with the common field cricket, or house cricket, belonging to the genus *Gryllus*.

Rearing crickets has come to be big business, and there are several cricket farms scattered throughout the country. Countless thousands of these useful insects are reared each year, for sale not only to schools and laboratories, but to zoos, museums, and game farms as food for reptiles and other insect eaters.

In raising crickets, it is better to establish several small colonies rather than one large one. With high population densities, crickets tend to die rapidly. This is especially true if any specimen contracts a virus disease—it will spread rapidly when the animals are overcrowded.

Another help in raising crickets is constantly to grade them for size. Young crickets are not at all hardy when kept under conditions optimal for adults. Young crickets drown themselves in the water dish needed for adults, and they are often eaten by the older and stronger insects. Cannibalism is greatly reduced if a bit of meat is added to the diet frequently, but there will always be some specimens that have an appetite for others.

According to Ward's Natural Science Establishment (one of the leading biological supply houses in the United States), an excellent food for rearing crickets is prepared as follows. Grind rolled oats, a little sugar, a little powdered skim milk, and water together to make a paste. A mortar and pestle is a very good implement to use for the grinding process.

Spread this paste in a thin layer on a sheet of heavy wrapping paper and let it dry. After drying, cut it into 1-inch squares and store it in a tightly sealed jar. The food will keep indefinitely, and the squares can be fed every two or three days to the crickets. The amount fed is, of course, dependent upon the number of insects you are feeding, and the amount of supplemental foods you give them. The dried paste should be supplemented with a few lettuce leaves, a small piece of meat (preferably cooked), grasses, dandelion leaves, celery, apple or any other fruit, potato—in fact, nearly anything is good food for these omnivorous insects. You must guard against mold forming on the moist foods; if this happens, remove the moldy food immediately. There should always be some dried paste food in the cage. Other foods should be removed each morning and replaced fresh at night—crickets feed at night.

A cage for crickets is simple enough. It should be not less than 12 inches high, or the insects will be able to jump out. If it is this high, no cover is needed, and this will help to prevent mildew and mold from forming. A small aquarium is ideal.

An old aquarium, even if it leaks, makes an excellent cricket cage.

An inch of sand should be placed in the bottom of the cage, and for small crickets, the sand should be dampened for moisture. Young crickets invariably drown in a water dish. For larger and adult insects, a shallow water dish is required. A jar lid is fine. Several flat rocks can be put on top of the sand to form hiding refuges for the creatures.

A layer of dead leaves on the sand is very helpful. They form perching places as well as places to hide from the light of day and from each other. As has been said, crickets cannot tolerate high population densities. Not more than 24 specimens can be kept in a 5-gallon aquarium, because even though the cubic volume of the aquarium is large, the cricket population can live only on the floor of the tank, limiting the living space to the square footage of the rather small container.

The population may be doubled, or even tripled, by the addition of layers of screening. Boxlike frames of window screen may be bent up to stand inside the tank, making them smaller than the tank area to permit the crickets to climb up around them on all sides. Additional boxes may be made to stand upon the first, making several stories inside the aquarium, counting the aquarium floor. Of course, when the inside is built up like this, the aquarium must be covered with a screening lid or the insects will be able to jump out and escape.

When building an apartment house in this fashion, be sure to place a food and a water lid on each floor. Otherwise there will be battles among the high population around a single source of food and water. Dead leaves can also be spread on each upper floor as well as on the bottom.

Egg separators can be used in place of screening, and these can be stood on edge instead of laid flat inside the cage. The screen levels can also be placed on edge if you like, in which case a water lid and feeding station can be placed on each side of the cage to afford better distribution and room for the insects to gather at them.

A bunch of clean excelsior in the cage also provides three-dimensional space for crickets, and enables you to

46

A female cricket, showing the long, thin ovipositor between the two rear points.

A male cricket, superficially similar to the female but with no ovipositor.

greatly increase the population density of each cage. Excelsior is also good material to use when shipping crickets, as it gives the insects good foothold while traveling through the mails. Put enough excelsior in the shipping box to prevent it shifting around, and the insects will crawl in between the strands, riding in comfort.

Crickets are normally creatures of the night, so sunlight is not essential. A dark, damp, hot location is suitable for their care.

Sexing these insects is a very simple matter. As you look down on them, the male has two fringed projections at the rear end of the abdomen. The female also has these appendages, but centered between them, she also has a long, spearlike ovipositor, projecting a considerable distance beyond the other two. There are other differences, but the ovipositor is so quickly and easily seen that it is not necessary to look for more.

47

With this ovipositor, the female lays her eggs underground in the fall. At the first hard frost she dies, as do the males. The eggs overwinter underground, hatching in the spring. This cycle can be broken by rearing indoors, where frost does not kill the adults, which will then live for a longer time and have several broods.

Crickets may be trapped with ease by the use of a very simple device. A large jar such as a Mason canning jar makes a good trap. The lid should be of the two-piece variety, having a ring that screws to the top of the jar and contains a flat inner disk. The disk is discarded, since the ring is all that will be used. A cone of window screening, preferably the plastic kind, is made to fit inside the opening of the jar. The cone may be fastened by sewing the seam with string or fine wire. The apex is cut off to leave a hole ½ inch in diameter, and the wide end must be wider than the opening of the jar. The cone is pushed into the jar, and the wide end is turned down over the outside of the top. Then the ring is screwed in place. If the ring will not fit over the screen to screw onto the jar, the cone may be held in place with a heavy rubber band.

Peanut butter is one of the best baits to use for most animals. Spread some on a crust of bread or a cracker and lay it inside the jar, placing the jar on its side in a location where you have either observed crickets or heard them chirping. Set the trap in the early evening, and leave it out all night. Besides peanut butter, you may use fruit, vegetables, meat, or almost anything, but you will find the peanut butter to work better than most other baits.

Crickets like it hot. As a matter of fact, they *must* have heat in order to survive and thrive. Ninety degrees is about optimal for rearing crickets, and, at this temperature, they will mature in about one month. At lower temperatures, the insects will take considerably longer to mature. However, they will live longer at lower temperatures, so the temperature you maintain them at depends upon the purpose you have for breeding them. For crash breeding to obtain quantities of specimens for sale, it follows that you will want to keep them at high temperatures in order to accelerate their maturation rate.

For breeding in quantity, a method of obtaining eggs is sometimes used that seems to produce better results than the method I have described above. The aquariums are not fitted with sand layers, but the bottoms are left bare, except for dead leaves. To provide a place for egg laying, small flat containers are used. These may be round, flat dishes of some kind, not less than an inch deep—culture dishes are ideal, or even small bowls. Fill these with clean, sterilized garden loam. The packaged garden soil sold in nurseries and supermarkets is perfect for the purpose. Sow the soil with grass seed, clover seed, wheat, rye, or almost any other grain. These dishes are placed in the cages and the soil watered enough to permit the seed to germinate.

The crickets will lay theirs eggs inside the dishes, under the surface of the soil. After laying is completed, the dishes can be removed from the cages and placed in the freezer for two or three days, not neglecting to keep the soil watered during that time, since the freezer will tend to dry it out otherwise.

After the dishes have been frozen for the proper length of time, they may be removed and placed in a regular refrigerator for about one month, still keeping the soil damp. The dishes may now be removed from the cold, and placed in a warm location—the warmer, the better; up to 90 degrees is best. Be sure you put the dishes in cages so the hatching nymphs will not disperse as they emerge from the ground. The eggs should hatch within two to three weeks after warming them. New dishes may, in the meanwhile, be installed in the original cages for new batches of eggs. If you work out the timing and maintain ideal conditions within all cages, you will soon be running a regular production line of egg dishes being laid in, being frozen, being refrigerated, and placed out to hatch. You are now on the way to maintaining an uninterrupted crop of crickets.

CHAPTER 7
Grasshoppers

With a few differences, rearing grasshoppers is much the same as rearing crickets. However, grasshoppers are even less tolerant of crowding than crickets. Also, grasshoppers are not as hardy as crickets, and often colonies of them will suddenly die out completely. This may be due to the fact that under conditions of confinement grasshoppers are prone to virus diseases that decimate the population overnight.

Grasshoppers can walk right up a sheer surface, so their cages must be covered at all times. Large galvanized ashcans make ideal grasshopper farms, if the covers are replaced with screening. Such a can will accommodate up to 100 adult insects. Naturally, you must use screen with a fine enough mesh to contain the young nymphs. However, if the method of breeding grasshoppers is the same as was described for breeding crickets—i.e., using egg trays and removing them for hatching—then the covers for the adult farms may be coarse ¼-inch mesh hardware cloth, which makes a more convenient cover, since the hardware cloth is stiff and holds its shape well. The young nymphs will be kept in separate cages with finer screens over them.

Grasshoppers are not quite as omnivorous as crickets.

CHAPTER 8
Mealworms

Perhaps more mealworms are raised for food for insectivorous animals than any other creature. They are extremely simple to raise and take up little space. The commonly raised mealworm (genus *Tenebrio*) is the larval stage of an insignificant beetle. Mealworms feed on any of the dry cereals, but wheat in some form seems to have the best results.

The plastic sweater boxes sold in all department stores are fine for mealworm farms. The covers are tight-fitting enough to prevent the escape of the insects but still permit the admission of air. They are usually about 11 inches wide by 16 inches long and come in two depths, 4 inches and 8 inches. The shallow ones do very nicely for smaller farms, and the deeper ones for larger populations.

The box is filled about ¾ full of clean, fresh cereals. It is a good idea to make up a mixture. Rolled oats, wheat germ, corn meal (either the white or the yellow variety), wheat bran, chick-growing mash, and other cereals available at feed stores all over the country are excellent for raising mealworms.

One condition will ruin a mealworm farm in short order: dampness. Mealworms simply cannot tolerate damp conditions. However, they must have some kind of moisture. This is easily supplied in slices of raw potato or apple.

A piece of burlap, dampened and rung out completely, is laid on top of the cereal, and on top of this sliced potato or apple is placed. The slices should be renewed every few days. A goodly number of mealworms introduced to the box will start the farm.

Mealworms may be purchased from biological supply houses or from local pet shops. If the pet shop does not have them in stock—an unlikely condition—they can easily get them for you. They are sold by the worm—usually for one cent each—or by the quarter-pound. One quarter-pound is a good amount for starting a farm. They are simply dumped in on top of the cereal, where they will immediately begin to burrow under the surface.

These insects undergo complete metamorphosis. That is to say they have four stages in their development: the egg, the mealworm, a pupal stage, and finally the beetle. The beetles do not generally fly, but crawl about, mate, lay their eggs, and soon perish thereafter. Strangely enough, animals that take mealworms eagerly as a main part of their food do not seem to relish the beetles. The pupae are eaten readily, but for some reason or other their beetles are not.

Mealworms are used as food for fishes, reptiles, and small animals. Zoos, museums, and game farms use them by the thousands, and they have a ready sale in whatever quantity you can produce. A hundred or so plastic boxes started with mealworms will after one year produce large quantities that will be readily salable to the local pet stores or zoos.

When the worms hatch, they are so tiny as to be almost invisible. They soon reach a size, however, where they serve as food for baby reptiles and baby fishes. The beetles are

54

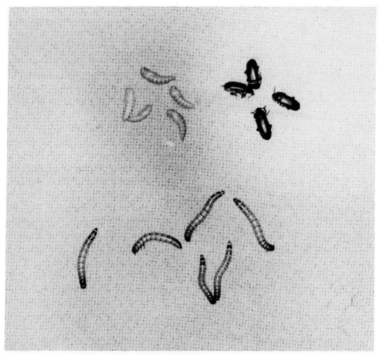

Three stages in the four-stage life cycle of the mealworm. At the bottom are full-size mealworms, about an inch long; when they hatched from the eggs they were almost invisible. Eventually they become pupae, shown at top left, and finally beetles, which lay eggs to begin the cycle again.

single-brooded. This means they lay eggs only one time before they die. However, in a going farm, the worms are of all different sizes and ages, so the crop is continuous. The egg-laying season extends from early May to late October. Worms from these eggs will be available from the end of November to the next spring, when they will pupate and metamorphose into beetles to begin the cycle again.

Mealworms prefer a cool, dark location. They do not require sunlight, and, indeed, full sunlight is detrimental to them. They cannot tolerate dampness, as stated before, yet should be kept in a cool place. Keep a close check on the boxes when they are first put in the location you intend to use. If any condensation appears inside the cover or on the sides, this must immediately be mopped up with a paper towel or tissue. The boxes then should be moved to another location where the danger of dampness condensing is eliminated.

After several months, depending upon the number of worms raised in each box, all the cereal will change into a fine grayish dust. This shows that it has all passed through the digestive tracts of the worms, and it should be changed at that time. It is easy enough to sift the cereal through a fine strainer, sorting out the worms, pupae, and beetles and letting the dust fall through.

However, you will lose a great number of eggs every time you sift it out. For this reason, it would be a good idea to sift the farm for renewal of the food at a time when not many beetles are present—or at least, when not many *live* beetles can be seen. This way, there is less likelihood of losing the entire crop of eggs. Even so, it might be a good idea to save the sifted dust, place it in another container for several weeks, and then sift it again. During that time, most of the eggs will hatch, and the second sifting will re-cover the young worms. They will be tiny, but nevertheless useful, since they will soon grow.

CHAPTER 9
Earthworms and Other Worms

Earthworms have two commercial uses. The first, and probably the most profitable, is as bait for fishermen. The second is as food for aquarium fishes; the worms are sold to a local pet store rather than directly to the customer.

Earthworms are fairly easy to rear, especially if you have an outdoor area where you can set up earthworm beds. It is far simpler to raise them outdoors than indoors, although they can successfully be reared indoors if you can keep them cool enough. Worms cannot tolerate temperatures above 58 or 60 degrees, and will quickly expire if the temperature reaches a point above 60. But if you have a cool, somewhat damp cellar you should have no trouble rearing the worms indoors. This is convenient during the winter, when outdoor beds would be inaccessible.

To prepare an outdoor farm, first examine the soil in your yard. If it is good loamy dirt, so much the better. If the soil is largely clay, then you will have to make other soil to fill the bed.

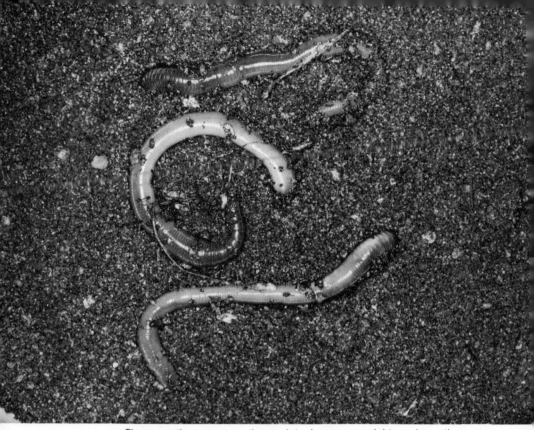

These earthworms are the variety known as nightcrawlers; they reach 6 to 8 inches in length.

Excavate a bed 6 or 8 feet square, to a depth of not less than 2 feet. If you live in a hard frost area, excavate not less than 3 feet deep. Remove all the soil from the area, with whatever tool is ready at hand—even a small backhoe can be used if you can rent one or have a contractor do the job for you. After the hole has been dug out, the side walls should be shaved true and square with a spade. The bottom should also be shoveled out level.

Now the excavation must be filled with prepared soil. If your soil is good you may use this with the other ingredients. If it is clay soil, then you will have to add half fine sand to it as you fill the bed. The mixture should include dead leaves, horse or cow manure, and shredded or chopped leaves from table vegetables such as celery, carrots, lettuce, beets, etc. Mix small quantities as you go—four shovelsful of soil (or two of clay soil and two of sand), one shovelful of dead leaves, and a handful of vegetable leaves, plus a shovelful of manure. Fill the hole in until the bed is once again level with the ground. The new soil mixture should be firm in the bed, but not packed down in any way.

Naturally, you would not have enough vegetable leaves from your own table stores to make a worm bed, but every supermarket, grocery store, produce store, or wholesale produce market trims vegetables daily, throwing out hundreds of pounds of leaves ideal for the worm bed. The store owner will be very glad, for the most part, to have you cart away the trimmings, since otherwise he would have to dispose of it himself. You might take several large plastic leaf and lawn bags with you when you go to the market, loading the trimmings in these to carry them without spilling them all over your car.

An easy way to mix the soil and manure is to use a cement mixer. These can be rented for a very small sum by the day, or maybe you have a friend who would loan you his. The proper proportions may be mixed and dumped directly into the excavation without further handling being necessary.

After the bed has been prepared, a starter culture of earthworms may be introduced. These may be purchased from a fishing bait store or from a biological supply house, or you may gather them wild by digging in damp soil for them. The worms should be covered with a thin layer of soil to protect them until they dig down deeper. Worms from the surrounding soil will migrate into a prepared bed also, to augment the population.

Every two or three weeks a layer of Pablum, corn meal, rolled oats, bread or cracker crumbs, wheat germ, or other fine cereal should be sprinkled on the surface of the bed and covered with a thin layer of sifted soil. The bed should be watered exactly as you would a lawn—well dampened, but not soaking, at least every other day during the summer months.

Before the first hard frost sets in, the bed should be

covered with a very heavy layer of dead leaves, or with hay or straw several inches thick, and boards should be laid over the covering to hold it in place. When the spring thaw arrives, the boards may be removed and the layer of leaves or hay turned into the soil, loosening the bed and aerating it at the same time. The regular feeding schedule and watering system may then be resumed.

Earthworms raised indoors are handled a little differently. They should be placed in large plastic, wooden, or metal boxes, filled with dead leaves. Ward's Natural Science Establishment claims nothing more need be added to the worm farm. There is nothing, however, against filling the worm farm with the black loamy potting soil available from supermarkets and nurseries, mixed half and half with the dead leaves. Also, celery, lettuce, or carrot leaves may be mixed in with the soil. Dry cereals may be sprinkled on the top of the soil, and the soil should be sprinkled often enough to keep it moist, but not wet. These animals can be raised in the house only if you have a place to store the farms where the temperature will not rise to 60 degrees. If you have no such area in your home, it is no use trying to raise earthworms. You are forced to do with the outdoor beds.

White worms known as enchytrae are used by many fish fanciers as a conditioning food for preparing the fish for spawning. These are fairly easy to raise if kept in a cool, dark location.

For cultures of enchytrae a plastic shoe box is a good size. This should be nearly filled with potting soil, dampened but not wet. Make a trench down the middle of the soil, and fill this trench with cooked oatmeal, Pablum, Wheatena, or Cream of Wheat. Let the cereal cool before adding the starter culture of white worms, then cover the worms and the trench with a thin layer of soil. Thereafter feed about once a month by sprinkling raw, dry cereal on the surface of the soil. Keep the culture moist, but do not flood the soil.

A cover should be put on the box to keep the moisture

in and to protect the worms from predators. The cultures must be kept cool and in a dark location.

At intervals, after the first six months to a year, the culture should be divided into two new cultures. In this way, population will be maintained at a better level than it would if you permitted the culture to continue to multiply without check.

Fecal worms resemble earthworms, but they are smaller and reddish in color. They are used mainly by laboratories, rather than as fish food or fishing bait. They are raised the same as earthworms, except that a much greater content of manure is required. Horse manure is best, but cow manure will also work. At least half manure and half soil should be used in the indoor as well as the outdoor beds.

Stock for starting the culture may be gathered around horse barns or at the piles of horse manure in the fields. Turn the manure over and you will see the worms under and within it. The same is true for cow pastures.

CHAPTER 10
Moths

In recent years, moth and butterfly pupae have been in great demand in laboratories and universities for scientific use. Serum cultures, virus studies, and many other projects require this stage of the butterfly and moth. Usually moth pupae are used because they are larger and because moths are easier to raise than butterflies. The butterfly is more difficult to rear mainly because of the special requirements of the adult insects in their mating procedures and because the eggs hatch in such a short time that it is difficult to get any from long distances or from other countries without them hatching in transit.

Laboratories use several species in particular. In this country the greatest demand is for cocoons of the Cecropia moth, the Io moth, the Polyphemus moth, and the Cynthia moth, and there is occasional demand for the cocoons of the Promethea moth. Schools and laboratories buy these cocoons in lots of several thousand of a kind, and have governmental grants to pay for them. Rearing moths in this quantity is a lot of work, and requires an enormous amount of food for the caterpillars.

The Cecropia, Io, and Promethea moths feed on wild cherry, while the normal food for the Polyphemus is oak, and that of the Cynthia is ailanthus. Most of these species will also accept other foodplants, but they do not do as well.

All you need to start rearing moths is eggs of whatever species you are rearing. Alternatively, you can start with a sexual pair of adult moths, attempting to get them to mate and the female to lay her eggs. In most of the species named, this is also easy. Any pair of moths will readily mate if given any opportunity. I have had Polyphemus moths mate while the female was sitting on the end of my finger! When the male mounted her, I transferred the coupled pair to a small twig, where they completed their copulation, remaining coupled for nearly four hours.

The best way to get adult pairs is to purchase cocoons from a breeder. Failing this, they can be trapped at a light set out after dark, with a sheet behind it. The moths are attracted to the light and alight on the sheet, where they may be picked off quite readily. The only problem is that the moth attracted to the light may be a male or a female, but it is difficult to get a pair at the same time. If the one attracted is a female, your job is easier, since you may tie the female out on a leash, and she will attract a male from as far away as a mile or more! The leash is merely a sewing thread tied around the body in a cross, under the wings. This, in turn, is tied to a piece of fly screen for a perching place, and the screen is hung up in a clear area outside. The female throws off scent scales that attract the males, and the mating follows as a matter of course. If the female you take at a light has already been mated, then she will fail to throw her scent. If after two or three days a male is not attracted, you may assume she has already mated. If she has been then she will probably lay her eggs all over the screen, and you will have achieved the desired result anyway, even though you did not witness a mating.

Eggs are also sold by the dozen by breeders all over the country, and this is really the easiest way to get started, except for purchasing paired cocoons and letting the moths

63

mate after emergence from the cocoons, at which time you will get several hundred eggs from each female. However, you must be certain that the pair couple, and actually copulate, or else the eggs will be infertile.

Female moths will lay their eggs within a certian time of emerging, whether or not they have actually mated with a male. They seem to be under a sexual urge to procreate, and the fact that a male has not coupled with them does not seem to matter.

If you are starting with adult moths, after the female has been fertilized she will commence to lay her eggs in a very short time. As soon as the pairing is over, the female should be placed in a large brown paper sack that has been opened up full. Confine the moth by folding the top of the bag over and holding it closed with a paperclip. The moth will lay her eggs in the sack, in patches. Leave her in the sack for at least two days to make sure she has laid all her eggs. She may now be released; you will find her wings battered and most of her scales rubbed off from the strenuous exertion of ovipositing. The eggs can now be cut out of the sack, leaving a small margin of paper around the patches. Make no attempt to pick the eggs off the paper. This can damage them, since they are stuck on quite firmly.

The paper patches containing the eggs are now placed in a small plastic box with a lid. If the lid fits very tightly, a few very small holes should be drilled through to admit air. Failing this, air can be admitted to the box by wedging a piece of thick paper under the lid when closing it, to leave a gap.

A small wad of cotton, not larger than a bean, is moistened with water and put into the box with the eggs, but not touching the eggs themselves. The wad should be remoistened daily. The eggs will hatch in about ten days if they are kept in a warm place.

Before the eggs hatch, you must make provision for feeding the tiny larvae after they emerge from the shell. As soon as you see the eggs beginning to hatch, place fresh leaves from the proper foodplant in the box. Do not try

A small-scale brooder for caterpillars made from a cardboard carton with a window of screening and a glass top. Fronds of vegetation project into the water through a hole in the bottom of the box and are changed as often as necessary.

to pick up the newly hatched caterpillars, or you will injure them. The tiny creatures hold fast instinctively, and any attempt to dislodge them from their support will damage them. It may even pull off the prolegs, since they will not let go their hold.

If you put the leaves near the young caterpillars they will eventually walk on them and begin to feed. Do not remove the empty egg shells after the eggs have hatched, because often the caterpillars will eat part or all of the shells as their first meal.

The food must be changed daily, to ensure its freshness. Here again, you are faced with the problem of moving the caterpillars from the stale leaves to fresh ones. The simplest way is to cut out a tiny bit of leaf with the caterpillar on it and drop this bit on top of the fresh leaf. The animal will transfer itself with no further urging from you.

Caterpillars undergo several instars or molts. This means they will molt their skins several times as they attain full growth, finally to pupate or make their cocoon according to the species being reared. (All of the species I have mentioned make cocoons.)

At the time of molting the caterpillar may stop feeding for a day or so, remaining still in one spot. Under no circumstances should you disturb it during this crisis. Particularly, do not try to transfer it from its perch on the old foodplant, because the caterpillar spins a tiny pad of silk on the leaf, to which it attaches its claspers in order to get a good foothold to draw out of its old integument. Breaking this foothold may prevent the animal from completing the molting process, and it will then die within its old skin.

After molting the caterpillar undergoes a very rapid increase in size, with an accompanying increase in appetite. At this time, you may have to move the batch to a larger cage. Cages for rearing caterpillars must be tightly closed. These insects are accomplished escape artists, and can ooze through a hole you would not think possible.

While it is quite possible to rear caterpillars on cut food indoors, you will be astonished at the difference in the size and well-being of the animals when reared outdoors on living foodplants. In order to accomplish this you have to devise some method of confining the larvae on the branch or the tree. While the caterpillars will not wander too far from a foodplant—in fact, they would be quite content to pass their entire lives eating from the same tree, finally making their cocoon on a branch, twig, or the trunk of that tree—they must be protected from predators, and that is the main purpose of confinement.

Moth and butterfly larvae are vulnerable to various predators. Wasps of many kinds parasitize them by laying their eggs in the living body of the caterpillar to later emerge and eat the host. Squash bugs and shield bugs suck the caterpillars dry, especially in the earlier instars. There are a multitude of everpresent birds on the lookout for a juicy tidbit either for themselves or to take to the nest as food for their young.

The best way of protecting your animals is to build screen cages large enough to enclose the entire plant. If the food-plant for the particular species you are rearing is a tree, perhaps you can find a young specimen, small enough to fit within a cage, yet large enough to support a population of caterpillars. Bear in mind that while they are young, caterpillars do not require a great deal of food.

After the second instar, however, when their growth increases in leaps and bounds, you will finally arrive at the point of desperation when you feel that the only way you can get enough food to them is with a pitchfork. The caterpillars get to be like sausages, with ravenous appetites, and a dozen of them can defoliate a small tree.

Another method of protection is to sew up large sleeves of plastic fly screening, with fabric ends. The fabric should be not less than 1½ or 2 feet long on each end of the screening, and the screening part of the sleeve as long as you can handle comfortably. Four to 6 feet is a nice size for an average sleeve.

In practice, a branch is selected that is well leafed out and free from small sharp twigs. If the twigs are present, then you should trim them away. They make it difficult to install the sleeves, and they may tear the sleeve itself, permitting the entry of predatory insects.

Before you sleeve the branch, it must be shaken vigorously for several minutes to dislodge any other insects inhabiting it. When you are satisfied that the branch is free from enemies you may install the sleeve.

The sleeve is slipped over the branch, and the inner fabric end is gathered tightly around the branch at the trunk side, then tied securely. Make certain the tying closes the fabric around the branch so tightly that no small insects can get through.

Now you may introduce the caterpillars, either by dropping them into the bottom of the sleeve, where they can find their own way to the leaves, or by placing them in among the leaves. If you are handling tiny, newly hatched larvae, you may simply pick up the leaves they are feeding on and place the entire leaf in the sleeve, wedged in among the growing leaves on the branch. The outer end of the fabric is now tied securely, enclosing the branch.

A sleeve may be placed on a branch, and the eggs put inside to hatch, so that the caterpillars can begin to feed directly on growing food. The paper patches can be attached to different leaves simply by pinning them to the leaf. When the eggs hatch, the little animals will find the leaf and start feeding.

At least every other day during the first three instars or molts, and then every day from then on, the sleeve should be cleaned of droppings. The droppings of caterpillars are small pellets, dry and without odor as long as they remain dry. If they are wet there is a smell, although it is not too objectionable. To clean a sleeve, you merely untie the outer end and shake out the detritus that has fallen to the bottom. Then retie the sleeve.

At the time of cleaning you may also inspect the branch. If there are still a good number of uneaten leaves present, leave it alone. If the branch is becoming stripped, you must transfer the sleeve to a new branch. The best way to do this is to install a new sleeve on the new branch, then pull the old sleeve off, pick off the caterpillars, and place them in the new sleeve. If the caterpillars are not feeding, but resting on a twig or stem, they may be spinning their molting pads, and you should transfer them by clipping the twig with them on it and putting the twig and all into the new sleeve.

When the caterpillars reach their final instar and the time comes for pupation, they evacuate their gut of all food, making a dark liquid splash. If this splash falls on leaves below them, and if there are caterpillars still feeding but not yet ready to pupate, you should remove the stained leaves, since eating them is bad for the caterpillars.

After evacuation, the caterpillar begins to wander restlessly about the sleeve or the cage, finally coming to rest in a location it feels suitable, and there it spins its cocoon. Inside the cocoon, the caterpillars' head falls off, thus triggering the pupation response, and within a few hours or days it has metamorphosed into the pupa. Do not disturb a cocoon for at least a week after it is completed. At that time, if you cannot leave them in place where they were spun up, you may carefully peel them away from their support and store them in small containers in a cool place. They should be dampened slightly at intervals throughout the winter, if you have not sold them all before then.

You may, from time to time, get an order for just male cocoons or female cocoons. It is easy to sex moth pupae. In cocoon-making moths, you must slit open the cocoon, taking care not to injure the pupa, to expose the pupa. Holding the naked pupa with the wing case on top, count down to the fourth segment below the wing case. If this fourth segment is in any way broken, indented, or otherwise interrupted in outline, the pupa is invariably female. If the fourth segment is intact, the pupa is invariably a male. Then put the pupa back in the cocoon, close it, and tape it shut.

CHAPTER II
Hellgrammites

If you have a stream running through your property, you are very fortunate, because the possibilities of putting such natural water to use are many. One excellent use is the raising of hellgrammites, which are the aquatic larvae of the dobsonfly. Hellgrammites are probably the best bait for bass fishing known.

The insect exists as an underwater larva for approximately three years. Your breeding stock must be taken wild, since there is no source that I know of that sells breeding insects. However, it is easy to catch hellgrammites, although it takes two people.

To make a hellgrammite trap, take a piece of plastic fly screening about 24x18 inches and tack the shorter sides to two stiff wooden sticks. This is the only equipment you will need, except for containers to carry your catch home in.

Find a good stream with rocky and muddy bottom, and, standing with your legs securely placed, hold the screen against the bottom as tightly as possible by grasping the two sticks in your hands. Your assistant should stand upstream about three or four feet. He will turn over the rocks, disturbing the bottom to make it wash down into your seine. As soon as the water has begun to clear, lift the net up and hold it horizontally while you examine the contents. With each pass you should have a hellgrammite or two. You may also have small crayfish and other aquatic insects and larvae, even small minnows at times.

Netting hellgrammites. Rocks are turned over a few feet upstream from the screen, then the screen is lifted and examined.

A hellgrammite caught in the screen.

A crayfish. Often caught when netting hellgrammites, crayfish make good bait too.

Put the hellgrammites in water-filled containers for transport to your creek. In the area you wish to use for breeding, a section should be partially dammed. This can easily be accomplished by scraping two paths about a foot wide across the bed of the stream, say 10 feet apart. Two old railroad ties make ideal dams, since they will serve as anchors for the cage to be added, and still permit free flow of the water over them, not actually damming the stream. Before the ties are lowered in place, bore a hole about 2 inches in diameter through each end, as far apart on the tie as the stream is wide. In other words, the holes should be just at each bank of the stream. Now place the ties in position, making certain that the bed of the stream is plugged tightly all along the bottom edges. For the time being, this is all you have to do to start your hellgrammite farm. You may now introduce your wild-caught stock. Remember that the period of aquatic life is three years, so you should catch as many of the wild insects as you can, and of all different sizes. Some will mature each year, and after a year or so, you should have a continuing supply of bait animals.

To keep your hellgrammite farm going, you will need the services of the adult stage of the insect. Dobsonflies mate in midsummer and lay their eggs on overhanging supports. As they hatch, the larvae drop into the water to begin their long sojourn beneath the surface. In the early spring, you should erect a mating cage. Now the holes you bored through the ties are put to use. Make two square U-shaped frames out of 1-inch galvanized pipe and elbows. Two elbows are needed for each frame, and two uprights about five feet long, threaded on one end only. A horizontal frame member as long as is needed to span the holes in the ties completes each frame. Screw an elbow on each end of the horizontal member, then screw in the uprights, finally pushing the frame down through the holes in the ties.

Over these frames you now stretch plastic fly screen. A log, a length of 4x4 lumber, bricks, or even heavy stones can be used as weights on the banks. The fly screening should touch both banks, with enough left over to permit positioning the weights along the edges. The ends should have flaps of screening reaching down to the surface of the water, or even a little below the surface. They can be held in place by placing stones along the edges on top of the ties.

If you cannot find screen wide enough to span the entire length of your cage area, you may tie two poles or pipes across the two frames, boxing in the top area. Then strips of screen can be cut to reach up from one bank, across the top, and down to the other bank. Lay strips with a 5-inch overlap.

Push several branchy shrubs inside the screened-in area and into the stream bed to provide perching places for the dobsonflies. The larvae that are ready for metamorphosis will burrow into the banks of the stream and pupate there, taking about one month for the transformation to the adult. As the flies emerge from their pupae, they will mate over the brook and lay their eggs, which will hatch and drop into the confined area. The screening must be weighted down along the stream banks to trap the emerging flies as they come out of the bank. Otherwise they would fly to other areas in the stream and you would lose the crop of eggs.

Ordinarily, enough natural food would be found in any stream to supply the needs of the larvae, but since you are confining an area and creating a population density far above that in a natural ecosystem, you should make some provision for extra food. This can be in the form of other aquatic insects and larvae, trapped the same way as was your breeding stock. If you collect frog's eggs and toad eggs and place the jellylike masses in the stream to hatch into tadpoles the hellgrammites will have an excellent source of food. Salamander eggs may be used the same way. These all are available in the early spring in small sheltered pools, in wet muddy holes, and in the streams as well.

A fine net may be used to catch tiny, newly hatched minnows, sometimes by the thousands during the spawning times in the spring. These little fish swim right at the shore, usually in the sun-warmed shallow water, in between large flat rocks and in shallow rills over the rocks, and they are very easy to take in almost unlimited quantities. Dumped into your area, many of them will remain in place without washing over your railroad-tie dam, to provide a lasting food source for the hellgrammites. The fish will be taken up to quite a large size by the larger hellgrammites. Your crop may be harvested the same way and with the same equipment used to trap the wild stock.

CHAPTER 12

Mantises

As diligent as man has always been in attempting to eradicate most insects from the face of the earth, he has neglected to enlist the aid of a wonderful ally except in very recent years. This is the marvelous praying mantis—one of the most voracious predators in the entire insect world. Nowadays the value of the mantis is recognized and it is protected to a certain degree.

A mantis will attack and eat anything that moves in the insect world, and it is capable of overcoming any other insect, regardless of its size. The mantis itself is no small insect, attaining a growth of nearly 6 inches.

The females are larger than the males, and their bodies are fatter and fuller—the body of the male is slender and pointed. Both insects can fly. Besides being voracious predators of all other insects, mantises are cannibalistic, eating each other with relish.

Many people throughout the country are making a sideline of selling mantis oothecas. An ootheca is an egg case,

Praying mantises mating. The female, already larger than the male and soon to grow much larger, will probably devour the male as soon as they have finished coupling.

and each one may contain as many as a thousand eggs. Usually oothecas are collected in the wild, but mantises can be reared very easily if you take the trouble to segregate each insect shortly after it is hatched.

Segregation can be accomplished by placing each individual insect in a container such as a quart mason jar, along with a branchy twig for the insect to rest upon. The lid should be perforated for air intake. As soon as the insects have attained growth enough to sex them, the males can be labeled so you know which is which when breeding time arrives. To breed the insects—they mate in late summer—the female should be placed in a cage about a foot square, with plenty of twiggy branches inside, and a male introduced. They should be closely watched. The female will either allow the male to mount her, or she will eat him. (There is a better than good chance that she will eat him anyway after he has completed his coupling with her.) If the female does not permit a mounting, a second male must

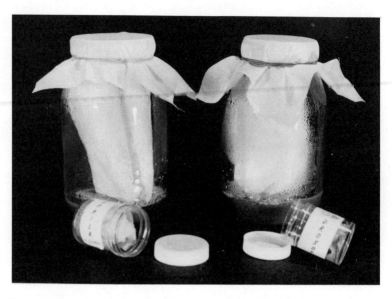

Two purchased cultures of fruit flies, genus *Drosophila*, came in the small jars and are being increased in the large jars.

be introduced, and this will have to continue until she tolerates the attentions of one of the males.

After coupling, the female will grow to enormous size, finally building her ootheca in the early fall. Shortly thereafter she dies, and the eggs overwinter to begin a new cycle in the spring.

The mature insects are not sold, but the egg cases are, usually for about 50 cents apiece or three for a dollar. They are purchased by gardeners and farmers. The eggs are placed among the flower or plant beds to hatch out, and the mantises prey on all insects in the garden. It has been discovered that a colony of these wonderful insects will keep almost all insect pests down in a flower or vegetable garden without damaging any of the plants themselves, because they are entirely carnivorous.

Mantises must be fed living insects. When they are first hatched, they cannot capture and eat such large insects as houseflies and cockroaches, but they are quite capable

78

of overpowering fruit flies. Since fruit flies are of great value to biologists for genetic research, they are available from biological supply houses, and almost any school science room will have a culture.

Once you have a starter culture of fruit flies you can raise them by the thousands in large jars such as instant coffee is sold in. The tops may be discarded, and a square of thin cloth like an old sheet or handkerchief is used as a cover.

A gruel must be cooked up for the flies to feed on in their larval stage. Enough for three jars can be made with ¾ cup of water, 1½ tablespoons of molasses, 2½ tablespoons of dry Cream of Wheat, Wheatena, or oatmeal, a pinch of salt, and a package of dry yeast. Bring the water, molasses, and salt to a boil in a small saucepan, then slowly sprinkle the dry cereal into the fluid. Stir until it begins to thicken, then pour it into the jars. As soon as the cereal is in the jar, sprinkle part of the yeast on top, then push a

Two shelves of fruit-fly cultures, each capable of containing thousands of flies.

folded paper towel down into the mush. Put the jar aside to cool thoroughly before introducing the starter flies.

Six or eight flies should be enough to put into each culture jar to start it going. Fasten the square of cloth over the top with a rubber band, and place the cultures in a warm— not hot—place to grow. Within a month you should have several hundred or even several thousand flies in each jar.

Fruit flies are not good specimens for rearing for sale, because they are so simple to rear that most laboratories and schools raise their own. Their real importance is as a source of food for your other animals—young reptiles, insects such as praying mantises, and tropical fish.

PART III
FISH

CHAPTER 13
Tropical Fish

It is difficult to know exactly what to call these creatures. In a book I wrote about them I called them "exotic fish," and was taken to task for the title because I had included fish indigenous to the United States in the work. In a series of articles done earlier, I called them "tropical fish," and was condemned because many of the specimens I wrote about were not from the tropics, but from more temperate waters. Whatever the correct terminology for the animals, here I will call them "tropical fish," which is the most common term.

Tropical fish are among the most popular living creatures raised in the home. From the beginning of the hobby of keeping these colorful little jewels in home aquariums, breeding in captivity has developed into the largest single enterprise in the hobby field. Millions of these treasures are bred every year, and each year sees more and more formerly unbred species successfully raised by a persevering fancier.

There are literally hundreds of different kinds of tropical fish for you to choose from. It would be impossible to pick any single species and say with any degree of veracity that it "is the best one to rear." You will have to be guided by your personal preferences, and by the purpose for which you wish to rear them. If you are interested in raising fish as a hobby, and for your own enjoyment and knowledge,

Angelfish are one of the most beautiful, and most salable, of tropical fish. This magnificent male is fanning his eggs, laid on a slate bar.

then almost any kind would do, except that I would say the egglayers are the most challenging and require more skill and knowledge than livebearing species do. These latter kinds are really not bred at all, since they go about their business of mating and dropping their young with no special preparation to speak of. As long as the water is the correct temperature, the food is sufficient and of the proper kind, and the fish are sexually paired, you should have babies aplenty.

Egglayers are another thing. These fish also require the proper foods in sufficient quantities, and the proper water conditions, as well as congenial ecosystems set up within their breeding tanks, but they themselves have to be brought into spawning condition by a little special care and attention before they will mate, lay eggs, and rear their fry.

With many species, telling the sexes apart is nearly impossible, and often a fancier will be overjoyed to find a large spawning of eggs in an aquarium, only to have them all be infertile. This happens because two females of certain species will spawn infertile eggs, caring for them just as though they were sexually paired. When the eggs finally show signs of becoming fungused, the fish will eat them.

Often, too, a pair of fish that are definitely of opposite sexes will mate and spawn, only to eat the eggs every time they lay them. When you have a truly magnificient pair of fish and this is the case, it is most disheartening, and the only thing you can do is to try to hatch the eggs away from the parent fish. Such is the case with a pair of angelfish in my home. The male is the most perfect and beautiful specimen I have ever seen in nearly thirty five years of fish raising, and the female is very little less. They spawn regularly, and eat every single egg the second day after laying them. Several times I have removed the eggs and hatched them in separate tanks, but one of the interesting things about rearing fish is observing the parental care given the young, especially in the great family of cichlids, to which angelfish belong.

If you intend to rear tropical fish for sale, then it is only good business to start with those that have a ready market and bring good prices. Angelfish are always in demand. So are the dwarf cichlids like rams, as well as the larger cichlids such as oscars. The oscar—*Astronotus ocellatus*—has several popular names, such as peacock cichlid and velvet cichlid, and commands high prices. A pair of breeders about 6 inches long will sell for $100 without any problem. Smaller ones sell for several dollars a pair, but, when buying a pair of oscars, you are not always certain you have anything other than two fish. It is most difficult to tell the sexes apart. Perhaps the best way to do so is to purchase six or eight young ones and raise them to maturity, at which time they will pair off themselves, and you can keep those pairs that mate separate from the others. Oscars get to be nearly a foot long, as they have enormous appetites. They require a very high protein diet, and mostly live food, like earthworms, mealworms, and insects. Beef heart is all right, and so is dog food, provided you use the kind that is not full of fat and oil, which could foul the water in the tank. Earthworms are perhaps the best food you can find to obtain fast growth and full health in oscars. If the earthworms are very large, they should be chopped into pieces. Sometimes the fish will eat dry food, but usually they take it only reluctantly. Nevertheless, some dry food should be offered to them daily.

Oscars require a large tank—not less than 50 gallons in capacity, and a 100-gallon tank is even better. It is useless to try to put fast growth and good fins on a large fish in a small tank. It simply cannot be done.

Since the early days of the hobby, when fish died for no apparent reason, it has finally become known that there are certain water conditions that must be met for the fish even to survive, let alone spawn and rear young. Temperature, of course, is a condition that is very evident. It is a matter of reason that temperatures should be correct, and this creates no great mystery in the mind of the fish fancier. The temperature of the water the fish is in must be adjusted to the temperature of the water it is being transferred to before the fish can tolerate the change. This is very easily done. After your tank has been set up and the water adjusted to the correct temperature, you get your fish—more than likely from the local pet store. They are brought home, probably in a small plastic sack with a small quantity of water. This water, while it is within the temperature range of tolerance for the fish, may be several degrees warmer or colder than the water in your tank. You simply float the container and the fish in the tank you intend them to occupy for not less than half an hour. The water in the container will very slowly reach the same temperature as the water in the tank, and then the fish may be emptied into their new home.

So much for temperature. Acidity is another thing. The acidity or the alkalinity of water is measured in degrees of pH, which denotes the hydrogen-ion concentration. pH is invisible, and there is no way of telling by looking at or feeling the water if it is acid or alkaline. As a matter of fact, the water may be drunk without being able to tell within several points if it is one way or the other. Yet the pH of water is one of the very necessary adjustments needed for the well-being of fish, and, indeed, in many species, for their very survival. Unless the water is at or very near the proper pH, the fish simply cannot tolerate it and will die within a short time.

There are many different kits on the market for testing water to determine the pH. A pH of 7.0 is neutral. Less than 7 the water is acid, and more than 7 it is alkaline. The pH of water can be adjusted by the addition of acid or alkaline solutions of sodium phosphate. This must be used within strict limits, and a great pH adjustment cannot be made quickly, but should be performed over a period of several days. A great pH adjustment means altering the pH more than, say, 0.3 to 0.5 degrees. An adjustment of 0.5 degrees should be the maximum. If the water requires further adjustment, you should do it in steps of 0.5 degrees spaced two to three days apart; the longer apart, the better. This is especially true if the fish are already in the tank. The rapid change could kill them just as surely as the incorrect pH. The concentration of sodium phosphate and the amounts to use for pH adjustments are indicated on the direction sheet that comes with each kit for pH measurement. However, it will do no harm to explain here how it is done.

Into one gallon of distilled water, dissolve 1½ ounces of sodium monohydrogen phosphate (Na_2HPO_4). This is the stock solution with which you can adjust water to the alkaline side.

For adjustment to the acid side, you make up a stock solution of one gallon of distilled water and 1½ ounces of sodium dihydrogen phosphate (NaH_2PO_4).

If your pH testing kit shows that the water is not the correct pH for the fish you want to rear, you must take a measured quantity of the water from the tank for your test in adjustment. One gallon is the most convenient quantity, and this amount is measured from the breeding tank into a clean container. Use whichever stock solution you need for making the water more alkaline or more acid. Keeping an accurate record of the amounts, add one drop at a time to the test gallon of water, mixing it in thoroughly, then testing it with your kit. When the test water arrives at the required pH, check the number of drops of stock solution it required to make the change, then multiply this number by the number of gallons in the breeding tank to find the total amount of solution needed to make the adjustment. As an example, say it took 10 drops to make the adjustment, and you are concerned with a 50-gallon tank. You will need 500 drops of the stock solution for the entire tank, *less the 10 drops you used for the test gallon,* since this water may be returned to the breeding tank.

If your fish are already in the tank, you must make pH adjustments very gradually—not more than 0.5 degrees every two or three days, as mentioned earlier. If you have a large quantity of gravel, rocks, or other ornaments in the tank, allowance for the volume of these must be made when calculating the quantity of water in making the adjustments. The average amount of gravel and a couple of good-sized rocks would occupy perhaps one gallon of volume, so the tank would measure that amount less than its rated capacity.

If you have not yet introduced the fish to the tank, the adjustment may be made in one addition, but in that case you should not put the fish into the water for at least a week or ten days, to give the chomicals in the water time to adjust and equalize. Be sure to test the water after the final adjustment has been made to make sure you still have the correct pH.

By listing all these precautions, I do not mean to give you the impression that tropical fish are such delicate creatures that they will roll over dead if you happen to sneeze in the same room as their tank. Some species are so hardy that they will live for years on end, and the lifespan of some of them is astonishing. All they require are the proper conditions, and pH and temperature are two of the most important of these conditions. Light is another factor that must be taken into consideration. A good rule of thumb to go by is that all aquariums should be in a more or less subdued light. Remember that fish, in their natural habitat, are under a great deal more water than they are in a tank in your home. This means that the light down where they live is much dimmer than the light glaring into their glass box from all sides and the top, too. Yet, fish do want enough light, and the plants kept in the tank with the fish also require light. This can be supplied by a reflector over the tank equipped with either a regular fluorescent tube or one of the Gro-Lux tubes developed especially for plant growth. Six to eight hours of light per day should be plenty. If algae begin to form in the tank, cut the time of lighting by two hours or so. A little experimenting will soon tell you the optimum amount of light needed to keep the tank in good operation, without turning the water green with algae.

Green water, by the way, is excellent food for the fry of some tropical fish. They are so tiny when born that they cannot eat anything much larger than bacteria, and green water is the first food you give them.

In order to *get* green water, merely put a tank in a place

where full sunlight falls upon it for several hours each day. The water will soon turn green, finally turning into a veritable soup of algae. A half-cupful of this water poured into the tank with the little fry supplies needed nourishment for them. A green tank will, after a time, clear itself. The algae will have consumed all the minerals in the water, and then starved to death. Once the water has cleared, it will remain so indefinitely. The water, after clearing from green algae, is usually crystal-clear, and this is the water to use when attempting to rear some of the more touchy fish.

In any event, the best thing to do when selecting a fish to breed for profit is to examine the market first. Go to several pet stores and price different kinds of fish. It is foolish to begin breeding fish that sell for only a few cents per specimen. Remember that the dealer is making a profit on them, too, so you are not likely to be able to sell your fish for more than half what the dealer charges. You will have all the work of breeding, plus the time and expense, for very small returns. It is as much trouble to breed inexpensive fish as it is to breed more expensive ones.

However, some fish that command very high prices do so because of the great difficulty of breeding them. It would be unwise, at least at the beginning, to try these either, except as a challenge to your ability in getting fish to spawn.

The medium-priced species are by far the wisest selection, and your pet store owner will be happy to tell you which of these are popular in your locality.

The next step is to get a couple of good books on breeding fish, and study the requirements of the species you select. Make sure, however, that you have a kind of which breeder pairs are available, or at least of which you can buy a lot to rear until they pair off. Selecting a rare breed to rear and then finding it unavailable is rather frustrating.

A very important item to take into consideration besides the price is the popularity of the species. It is far wiser to rear species that are in constant demand than to rear rarities that are not very popular even though they can occasionally bring much greater prices.

CHAPTER 14
Game Fish

Trout and bass, both important food and game fish, are reared in enormous numbers for stocking other waters that may have sparse populations. In various parts of the country there are establishments that offer fishing to tourists, with catches guaranteed. Usually these are large ponds, either natural or manmade, that have been stocked with fish for sport. Bass are more commonly reared than trout because they live to advantage in ponds and lakes, while trout prefer the cold running water of streams and rivers. True, there is a species of lake trout, but these inhabit large cool lakes, and grow to enormous size. The record for lake trout taken on a line is 63 pounds! The species of trout most commonly used to stock new waters is the brook trout, a much smaller fish; the record weight is about 15 pounds and anything over 5 pounds is exceptional.

Eggs may be obtained from hatcheries and introduced into your stream or pond for hatching. Eggs of brook trout

A man-made pond, suitable for stocking with bass.

require cold water for hatching. They will hatch in about six weeks at 50 degrees, and in three months at 40 degrees. The fish can tolerate temperatures up to 75 degrees, but do not do very well much higher than 60 degrees. Fingerling trout may also be purchased from state or private hatcheries, and these, of course, are much easier to bring to maturity.

Bass may be stocked in ponds either by introducing the eggs or by catching wild fish and releasing them. Wild bass caught on a hook and line may be saved for stocking by carefully removing the hook and keeping the fish cool while you transport it to the new location. Remember that fish crowded together in a bucket or other container will not survive more than an hour or so. It is a good idea, if catching bass for stocking, to do so during the summer months, then leave them alone to acclimate themselves to the new location; they will spawn in the spring with no further at-

Two- or three-day-old catfish can be caught in the hands and used to stock a pond.

tention. If the pond you are stocking with bass or trout is manmade and newly created, an artificial food supply will have to be introduced with the fish or the fish will be unable to survive. Bait minnows are good food for bass, and these may be purchased from bait stores or trapped yourself.

Ponds for stocking should not be too small. Half an acre is the barest minimum. The depth should be from one foot to 10 or 15 feet to enable the fish to survive over the winter. Sheep droppings or other manure should be put in the water in the spring and the fall to ensure good bacterial growth. The bacteria provide food for the small animals upon which the small minnows feed, to keep a steady food chain going for the larger game fish. Minnows introduced in the pond in the spring stand a better chance of survival than those put in in the winter, because insects will be hatching out in the water to supply them with food. Dry fish food may also be dumped into the pond to start a food chain for the bait fish.

Aquatic plants planted in the shallows will provide refuges for the minnows and places for them to spawn. This is important if you wish to establish a continuing food chain. Otherwise the bass will eat all the minnows and then starve.

Several cultures of daphnia, obtainable from your local pet store, poured into the pond after it has been fertilized with sheep manure should rapidly multiply and will provide an ideal live food for the minnows. After the minnow population has been established, daphnia may be hard to raise in the water, because minnows will eat them before they have a chance to multiply, but for the first season they will work wonders, and possibly enough will escape to form a small but continuing food supply.

If you have a cool stream on your property, heavy screen weirs can be stretched across the stream bed as far apart as practical, and the water in between used as holding places for trout. The fingerlings may be put inside the weirs, and they will grow to maturity provided they find sufficient food. You may have to augment the food supply with insects,

93

Trout require cold, running water, so to propagate them holding pools must be established in the bed of a stream.

ground beef heart, dog or cat food, earthworms, or almost anything else in the meat line provided it is ground fine. Such an arrangement is not good for actually raising trout, but is ideal for putting on some growth or for holding them for stocking other waters. Very small minnows are good food for trout, and as many of these should be added to the holding pond as you can manage. If the mesh of your weirs is large enough to allow the minnows to escape, you can add a finer mesh strip from the water surface down to the bed, and this will contain the food fish.

94

PART IV

SMALL MAMMALS

CHAPTER 15
Mice and Rats

White mice and white or black rats are very important research animals, ranking with hamsters in their usefulness to science. Rearing these rodents is no great problem if you can stand the smell. Mouse and rat urine is very high in ammonia, and they urinate constantly. So when you rear these animals for profit, your rearing area will soon take on an ammoniacal stink that becomes nearly overpowering.

In spite of this drawback, mice and rat rearing can be a profitable business. There are many rodent farms in the United States, some of them quite extensive. Huge barns have been converted into rearing establishments, where as many as 150,000 mice and rats, at any given time, are put through the production lines.

Mice and rats are reared in an exceptionally clean environment and are sold in several different stages, from "weaners" up through breeder size. Rodent farms not only sell the young vigorous animals, but sell the retired breeders after they are too old to have full healthy litters of young. These breeders are sold for 25 cents each for mice and $1.60 each for rats, for food for reptiles and other meat-eating animals.

White mice in a commercial breeding cage.

Rats are bred the same way as mice, the only difference being that their accommodations must be larger.

The white mice reared for scientific purposes are an albino strain of the ordinary house mouse, *Mus musculus.* House mice will readily interbreed with the white mice. They are of Asian origin, introduced throughout the world on ships calling from port to port. They now inhabit nearly every part of the world, from the Arctic to the tropics. Since mice are carriers of virus infections that attack man, it is better not to permit house mice to run freely in the house but to trap them if you find any evidence of their presence. Mice are one of the most important foods for many groups of animals. Hawks and owls—all birds of prey, in fact—eat mice as the major part of their diet. Snakes and large lizards, all crocodilians, and zoo animals such as the various species of cats all eat mice with relish.

The life cycle of mice is fairly short. They have a gestation period of nineteen days. Their eyes open two weeks after birth, and they are weaned at one month. In two months they are ready to breed, and at a little less than one year they are old. Mice have been known to live for several years, but these are exceptional animals, and they are too old to breed after about a year. The average litter is from four to six young, and the average number of litters per year is eight. Thus, a healthy breeder female can be counted on to produce approximately forty young before she is retired from breeding. Mice and rats are quite easy to sex; the testicles on the males are very evident.

Mice are sensitive to bright light, and should never be subjected to full sunlight. They are essentially creatures of the night, and even a few minutes of hard sunlight can kill them. This, and the fact that they must have ample warm nesting material, is responsible for most of the deaths in breeding mice. If plenty of material is supplied the breeding pair from which they can fashion their nest, and if the cages are kept in dimly lighted areas, all other factors being equal, your mortality rate should be practically zero among the babies.

Cages for breeding should be not less than 8 x 10 inches in area and 6 inches high. This is a handy size, and mouse breeding cages of these dimensions are commercially available, made of plastic and supplied with sliding top covers with a well for the water bottle and a grille top for the admission of air. Racks are also available to stack these cages. A large commercial mouse farm may have racks containing tens of thousands of cages, in rows several cages high.

A cage of these dimensions may house a group of six mice, three pairs. They will build individual nests and have their litters. However, it may be easier to breed them in smaller cages, say about 6 x 8 x 6 inches, and, when the young are weaned, transfer them in batches to the larger cages to pair off and mate. A gravid female may then be removed to a smaller nesting box when it is seen that she is getting ready to deliver her young.

Boxes for rearing mice can also be made of wood or metal, with covers of ¼-inch-mesh hardware cloth. A rack for the water bottle may be made of a small square of the same hardware cloth bent into a tent shape to support the

98

White mice kept as pets in an aquarium with wood shavings.

bottle at a slant. The tube from the bottle should be long enough to reach down to within about an inch from the floor of the cage. The animals may then reach the water supply without difficulty.

Whatever kind of cage is used, the floor should have a covering of pine shavings or commercial litter. One of the best commercial litters is called Cat Comfort, manufactured by the Georgia-Tennessee Mining & Chemical Co. of Atlanta, Georgia. This is treated clay material, very absorbent, and easy to use.

Mice urinate almost constantly. This is the reason they contaminate things in homes. They urinate on the food as they eat, and, if that food is an item of human food and you are unaware that a mouse has been nibbling at it, there is the possibility of your becoming ill from one of the many diseases carried by wild house mice.

In captivity, laboratory mice—the pure strains of disease-free albinos—do not harbor disease, and contamination is not the problem. What you are contending with is the ammonia smell from the accumulated urine. The shavings or Cat Comfort should be changed daily if possible and surely not less often than every other day.

Water bottles should be washed and refilled with fresh water daily. Food must also be constantly available. Mouse pellets are made and sold in quantity, or pellet dog food can be used. Mice will also eat—and they should have included in their diet—raw carrots, apple, potato, and most other vegetables or fruits. These should be given in small quantities, however, and the uneaten food should be removed from the cages daily to avoid contamination of the uneaten part. Grains and bird seed—especially wild bird seed—are acceptable too.

Pellets are usually contained in small boxes made of ¼-inch mesh hardware cloth, suseepended from the side of the cage about 2 inches off the floor. By suspending the food in this fashion, contamination from fecal matter or urine is avoided, and the animals will nibble the pellets through the mesh. Leftover pellets in such feeders do not have to be discarded as does any food offered in a dish in the cage. It is not enough merely to empty food dishes, refill them, and replace them. The dishes must be thoroughly washed as well.

The rats most commonly bred for laboratory purposes are an albino strain of the common Norway rat, *Rattus norvegicus*. The rat, like its smaller relative the mouse, originated in Asia, and has spread throughout the entire world.

The average life of the rat is from eighteen months to three years. The females seldom reproduce after eighteen months, however. The gestation period is about twenty-one days, and the young—averaging ten in a litter—are weaned three weeks after birth. The rats reach breeding age at three months, and they continue to breed for about a year.

Shredded newspaper, from which the female will make her nest, should be supplied in the breeding cages. When the female is ready to deliver her young, the male should be removed from her cage. After she has weaned the litter, she and the male may again be put in the same cage to breed again. The female should be disturbed as little as possible after the young are born; otherwise she may kill them in her anxiety over interference.

While most rats bred for laboratory purposes are gentle and make no attempt to bite when handled, take precautions when you are first becoming acquainted with these animals, because a rat bite is a serious matter. They are painful and usually bloody affairs, and there is always the possibility of infection. Large rat-breeding establishments hire people to do nothing but handle the rats daily. These handlers keep the rats so tame that they can be handled with no danger of a bite. This is an important factor where hundreds or thousands of rats are handled daily.

Food for rats is the same as for mice, and water bottles should be used in the same fashion as with mice. Water dishes can be used for rats if they are suspended from the side of the cage well off the floor and if they are small enough so that a rat cannot climb into them.

Cages are commercially available for rearing rats, as they are for rearing mice. Naturally, the rat cages are larger, about 10 x 12 inches in area and 10 inches high. The covers are provided with wells to hold the water bottle and food. The female rat, when ready to deliver, should be placed in a different cage with the shredded newspaper for nest building. She can be left in this cage until she has weaned her litter. Cages about 24 inches square are good for holding cages after the young have been weaned. Such cages will hold about eighteen half-grown rats or from six to eight adults.

Rats cannot tolerate overcrowding without undergoing drastic psychological changes. If they are being reared for sale to laboratories and hospitals, you must be careful to avoid excessive population densities, dividing the rats into smaller groups in cages large enough to permit the establishment of territories and dominance order.

Food for rats is sold commercially in the form of cubes.

They should be fed in baskets made of hardware cloth, but the mesh of the cloth should be larger than that used for mouse pellets. Keeping the feed boxes suspended eliminates the possibility of fecal contamination.

The optimum temperature for rearing both rats and mice is from 75 to 78 degrees. Colder temperatures slow the maturation rate, and subsequently the reproduction rate, while hotter temperatures speed up the metabolic rate so much that the animals become nervous, constantly hungry, and irritable.

Rodent farming can be a big business. The Blue Spruce Farms, Inc., in Altamont, New York, rears two strains of rats. One is pure white—albino—and is called the Sprague-Dawley strain. This strain has been bred at this farm since 1954, from breeders specially selected and isolated from other strains. The other rat breed is called the Long-Evans strain, and it has been bred at Blue Spruce Farms since 1963 from stock obtained from the University of Rochester.

Blue Spruce Farms began over twenty-five years ago when Mr. Ralph Plauth started to breed rabbits in wooden boxes in his old garage. After a few years he discontinued rabbit raising in favor of mice and rats, and the farm has grown in the last twenty years to be one of the most important rodent farms in the United States, with an investment of well over a million dollars.

Often a laboratory will require rats or mice that can be guaranteed to be free from pathogenic contamination. Under extreme sterile techniques, in specially built rooms, selected rats are bred and delivered of their young by hysterectomy/hysterotomy. The caesarean litters are then reared by foster nursing mother rats that have been handled under sterile conditions, and all are maintained in special rooms with filtered air, sterilized equipment, and masked attendants.

CHAPTER 16
Gerbils

Every once in a while people in one country will take an animal that is nothing more than a pest in another country, and make a pet out of it. The fad will catch on, and tens of thousands of the creatures will be carefully tended and cherished in their newfound havens. Such a case is the gerbil, *Meriones unguicucatus.* This is nothing more than the field mouse of Asia, India, and Mongolia. In their native lands, they sometimes abound in such numbers as to cause famines, killing tens of thousands of human beings by eating every stalk of grain in the fields. Such a famine took place in India in 1878, when the gerbils swarmed in such numbers that they literally denuded the land over an area of 8,000 square miles. Such numbers of animals is hard to conceive. Every stalk of grain was consumed, and all other vegetation eaten as the horde crossed the land.

Still, the gerbil has a place in the world, and many of them are making their contribution to humanity by serving as experimental animals in laboratories and schools over the land. Because they are really desert animals, many pet stores, and even some animal authorities, tell you that they

A group of gerbils in their cage. They are very tame and make no attempt to escape when the door is open.

can go for months without water and that it is not necessary to give them water at all, because they will get their moisture from their food. Perhaps gerbils can go months without water, but if you intend to breed them and keep them in peak condition, I strongly recommend that water bottles be placed in all the cages. You might be surprised to find out how frequently these animals who supposedly live without water intake will drink from the tubes.

Another fallacy is that it is not necessary to clean gerbil cages, on the theory that since they do not drink water, they do not urinate, hence there is no smell in the cages. Just the same, you should clean the cages not less often than once a week, discarding the litter and adding fresh. The litter can be pine chips or cat litter; in the breeding cages, wood chips are better because they form a better bed for the young.

The gestation period for gerbils is about twenty-five days, and the young are weaned in about thirty days. They are adult and ready to breed in ten to twelve weeks. The litter can contain as many as fourteen young, and they will breed every ten to twelve weeks.

Food consists of seeds (watermelon, pumpkin, sunflower,

birdseed), any grain such as corn, wheat, rice, oats, or rye, chicken scratch feed, and almost any fruit or vegetable. Fruits and vegetables should be offered only in small quantities, and leftovers should be removed from the cages each day.

Gerbils prefer to pick their own mates, and it may be difficult to get a pair to accept each other simply by dumping a male and a female into a cage together. It is easier to place a number of both sexes in a large mating pen, and watch them to see which of them pair off. Once they have paired to their satisfaction, the pairs may be placed in the individual cages to breed and rear their young. The adults may both be left with the young. Gerbils seldom molest their own babies. A female will mate and begin to gestate a new litter while she is busy nursing and weaning her first. By the time the second litter is near delivery, the first will be weaned and may be removed to another cage, or to the mating pen, to pair off for starting new colonies.

Hay, especially timothy hay, is relished as food by gerbils, and they will also use it to make nests. They will also use burlap. If you place several 6-inch or 8-inch squares of clean, new burlap in the cage, the adults will shred every single fiber of it into a fluff inside of which they make a nest. This fluffed burlap makes an ideal nest because it is good insulation, keeping the baby gerbils warm and dry.

Cages for rearing gerbils should be not smaller than 10 x 14 inches in area and 8 inches high. Commercial rat breeding cages can be used to advantage. Gerbils are rather hardy animals and are not prone to respiratory ailments or other diseases, but they should be housed in draft-free locations, and the temperature should be held around 75 to 80. Low humidity is best for them, since they are desert animals.

Besides being in demand in ever increasing numbers in universities and laboratories, gerbils are excellent food animals for snakes and other reptiles, and zoos and animal farms use considerable quantities. In small quantities, of course, these interesting animals can be sold as pets.

CHAPTER 17
Hamsters

It seems as though all the small animals come from Asia. The hamster is no exception. It abounds in Asia and Syria, sometimes in great numbers. The hamster is a quaint little tailless animal with very short legs and a roly-poly appearance. It has cheek pouches in which it stores food. It is one of the cleanest of the small animals, and is sometimes used as food in Asia.

Raising hamsters has become a sideline business for a great many people. It is easy to rear them, they are very prolific, and there is an increasing market for them to laboratories and schools, as well as to pet stores.

Cages for hamsters are the same as for rats. However, it is better to breed hamsters in trios rather than in pairs. The trio is composed of two females and one male. If the cages are made of wood, the screening, which can be ½-inch-mesh hardware cloth, should be placed on the in-

Hamsters are easy to rear and are so tame they make excellent pets.

side to cover all the wooden surfaces. Hamsters gnaw a lot, and would soon chew holes through an unprotected wooden cage. A nesting box, 6 inches square and 6 inches high, should be provided in the cage for each female. The top should be hinged, and there should be a circular opening in the front about 2½ inches in diameter and 3 inches off the floor. Dried grass, hay, shredded paper, or dead leaves should be provided for nesting material. Place some in the nest and the rest in the cage, and the females will use it to build the nest the way they want it. Cages should be kept in a warm, dry location, free from drafts and chilling winds. Hamsters do not like sunlight, being essentially a burrowing animal, and direct sunlight can kill them in a short time.

Hamsters require a high-protein diet, and if this is neglected by their breeders, they will eat their young in order to

107

gain the needed protein, or may even resort to cannibalism among adults. This may be averted by including protein substances as additives to their diet. Mealworms and other insects such as crickets and grasshoppers are excellent sources of protein. Wheat-germ oil added to their dry rations is beneficial to the pregnant females. Small pieces of raw meat can be offered, but take care to remove all leftovers at the end of each day to prevent spoilage and contamination.

Cooked liver is also good, and any green vegetables like cabbage, lettuce, carrot or beet tops, and also carrots themselves and grains and cereals. Commercial pellets with a high protein content are the staple diet, supplemented with the green vegetables. Bread soaked in milk is an excellent addition to the daily ration and could be offered two or three times each week, especially during the time of rearing the young.

The average litter in hamsters is eight to ten, but they can have up to fifteen young at a time. The gestation period is sixteen days, and the young are weaned in about two weeks, but they should be left with the mother for about four weeks. At six weeks of age the females are ready to be bred. The best age for sale is one month. The life span is about two and a half years.

In commercial breeding establishments, the females are retired from breeding after producing five or six litters. They are then usually sold to pet stores as pet animals, although this limits the life of the animal, since most of it was over as a breeder. If you sell retired breeders you should tell the pet store that that is what they are, and the approximate age of the creatures.

Often a pair of hamsters fight when placed together for mating. If this happens, they should be separated and then brought together again in about two days. Meanwhile, another female may be tried, and the first female may also be offered to a different male. Alternatively, several males and twice the number of females may be placed together in a large community mating cage, and observed until you are satisfied that the females have been properly mated. Each female can then be placed in its breeding cage to bear its young and raise them.

Wood chips or cat litter should be kept on the floors of all cages, and renewed every week, or oftener if necessary. Water is supplied in dropper bottles, held in place on the outside of the cages, with the tube close enough to the floor—about 3 inches—so the animals can reach it without stretching.

Hamsters do not respond to much handling or traffic around their cages, and for this reason they should be bred in an area where the only people walking around are those taking care of them. Loud and sudden noises may make the female so apprehensive that she will kill her young, or a pregnant female may either abort the young or have them stillborn. If you have outdoor space available that is free from public interference and from marauding dogs or other animals, hamsters can be reared very well there, provided there is a side or top shelter erected over the racks of cages to prevent drafts.

Metal commercial cages held in racks of eight or ten are ideal for rearing these little animals, and the same cages are useful for rats and guinea pigs. Of course, the cages must be brought indoors in the fall, or when the night temperatures begin to drop too low. Outdoor cages must be protected from rain. The animals should never be permitted to become wet, since this is apt to cause pneumonia.

Sexing hamsters is a problem to the uninitiated. The sexual apparatus is not as visible as in rats, mice, and other small animals. The easiest way is to look down at their rumps from above. A female has a fat round rump, while a male has a triangular pointed rump.

Because of their sensitivity to noises, hamsters are used extensively in research laboratories in exprimentation on the effects of tranquilizers. Also, hamsters are susceptible to more diseases of man than other experimental animals, making them more and more valuable as research animals.

109

CHAPTER 18
Guinea Pigs

Often a creature is given a popular name that has no found-
ation in fact. In the instance of the guinea pig, the animal
neither comes from Guinea, nor is it a pig. Actually it is a
cavy, indigenous to the high Andean slopes of Peru, where
it is esteemed as an article of food.

Since their importation as experimental animals, guinea
pigs have also been found to make ideal pets for children,
because of their gentle habits. They seldom try to bite,
although they are capable of doing so, and in rather a
fierce fashion. Several artificial strains have been bred into
the original line, and these are used as pet stock and for
shows. Perhaps the most striking pet animal is the long-
haired Angora or Peruvian guinea pig, and these command

The common, or English, guinea pig.

high prices in pet stores. The Abyssinian guinea pig also has long hair, though it is considerably shorter than the hair of the Angora. The Abyssinian's hair grows in swirling cowlicks all over the animal's body, giving it a quaint appearance. The English guinea pig is the ordinary short-haired strain. How it came to be called "English" I do not know. "Peruvian" would certainly seem to be more exact, since the wild stock, still living in the Andes, is also short-haired.

One disadvantage the guinea pig has as an experimental animal is that it seldom has more than two or three young at a time. Six offspring is unusual, but it does occur at times. Since hamsters, mice, rats, and rabbits all breed more freely and have much larger litters, they are rapidly replacing guinea pigs as laboratory animals, but the guinea pig still has a position in this field. Another disadvantage in rearing guinea pigs is that they require the addition of vitamin C to their diet. This, however, can be provided by the use of special foods as described later in this chapter.

Advantages are that the guinea pig, like the gerbil, is generally a healthy, disease-free animal, and also the guinea pig lives for several years—between seven and ten years is not at all unusual.

If you intend to breed laboratory animals, then you should specialize in the common shorthaired species. The other varieties are reared only as pet animals; as mentioned before, the Angora brings the highest prices—up to $10 each for good stock.

This valuable Peruvian guinea pig has such long hair that it is difficult in this view to tell which end is which.

Gestation in guinea pigs is from sixty-one to seventy days. Weaning takes about three weeks, and females can be bred at about five or six months. One male—males are called boars—will service up to six females—called sows—and this number and distribution may be kept together in one large breeding pen. The females will usually get along well together, even nursing one another's young if they have all delivered at approximately the same time. The young are born with their eyes open, and within a very short time they are running about. The females will mate again within a day after delivering. As soon as the young are weaned, they should be removed to growing pens and the sexes separated; otherwise the females will all be mounted by the time they are a month old. Guinea pigs may be bred at one month, but it is better for their health and well-being if they are kept segregated until they are older. The females of one litter should be bred to males from another litter, not from the same stock. In this way, excessive inbreeding is avoided, although such inbreeding for one or two generations does not seem to weaken the stock, and sibling matings are common. When the young reach near-maturity, the males should also be separated, since males will fight among themselves.

When the females are approaching their time of delivery, the diet should be augmented with bread soaked in plain milk, or in Similac with iron—a prepared infant food available in all grocery and drug stores.

Recommended sizes for guinea-pig cages are 30 x 36 inches in area and 18 inches high. This will accommodate a colony of six females and one male, with room for the females to nest and give birth to their young. If each cage has a sliding solid floor, which may be removed for easy cleaning, the cages may be stacked three or four high. If this is done, the cages can be screened on three sides, with the fourth side left open, and one door made of ½-inch-mesh hardware cloth can be hinged to close the entire battery. The animals do not attempt to scamper free if the cage is opened.

112

The floors should be covered with a layer of pine chips or cat litter. A small box may be provided for each female as a nesting place, and this should be filled with clean hay, which the animal may nibble as well as use for nesting material. Water and feeding boxes should be suspended from the sides of the cages about 3 inches off the floor, and water and food should be fed fresh daily.

Guinea pigs are vegetarians, but almost anything is accepted: grains such as wheat, corn, and oats, raw vegetables like lettuce, carrot, potato, corn, and fruits such as apples and pears. A salt block is a source of great pleasure to a guinea pig, and is beneficial to them as well. Grasses, dandelion leaves, plantain, and clover are relished, and in the summer months should be fed in quantities to augment the regular diet. Commercial guinea-pig pellets fortified with vitamin C are available, and the use of these pellets ensures the inclusion of the necessary vitamin in their diet. The pellets are dated, because the vitamin deteriorates, and the food should be used before the expiration date. Rabbit pellets can also be fed to guinea pigs, but they do not contain any of the needed vitamin, which then must be obtained from the fresh green vegetables listed above. Ascorbic acid tablets (vitamin C) may be added to the drinking water, if necessary, or they may be powdered and sprinkled on wet foods such as apple or potato or mixed with the dry cereal foods. All foods should be fed from feeding boxes or hoppers suspended from the side of the cage to prevent contamination with fecal matter or urine. A small amount of cod-liver oil added to the food is very beneficial to guinea pigs, improving their coats and overall well-being.

Temperature requirements are not too rigid, although 65 degrees is the lowest they should be forced to endure or they may contract pneumonia or other respiratory ailments. About 75 degrees is the best temperature. Guinea pigs also require a rather high humidity, about 55 percent, so if you are intending to rear them in quantity, a humidifier will almost be a necessity in the breeding room.

CHAPTER 19

Rabbits

I am sure that no one needs an introduction to rabbits. They have become almost a universal pet animal, and are also raised in great quantities as a source of meat. Europeans use rabbit meat much more than do Americans, but it still is marketed in significant quantities in this country. Rural people are far more familiar with eating rabbits than are citydwellers. Fried rabbit is difficult to distinguish from fried chicken; the main difference is the shape of the pieces.

Besides being an important food animal, rabbits are raised for their fur, which, besides being offered as what it is—rabbit fur—is clipped, sheared, and dyed to simulate many other furs. The sheared hair from rabbits is as important, since it is the material from which top-quality felt is made. While the fur of rabbits is not very durable, its cheapness makes it popular for extensive use. It has a number of trade names, none of them giving any clue to to what the fur really is: clipped seal, polar seal, arctic seal, cultured chinchilla, and many others.

A shorthaired pet rabbit.

Of all the varieties, perhaps the most beautiful—certainly the most luxuriant—is the chinchilla rabbit. This strain was bred to look like the true South American chinchilla, and its fur is long, silky, and a beautiful steel-gray in color. Next in beauty is the Angora rabbit, with the same kind of long silky hair, but in pure white or solid colors. Wool is obtained from the Angora strain. The hair of Flemish Giants and New Zealands is used for felt by the hat industry.

Next in the line of importance is rearing rabbits as pet animals. Rabbits are usually tame and docile, and have been bred into countless color strains, offering a variety unparalleled in any other species. Rabbits are raised by school children for biology projects, and for farm fair exhibits. And, being prolific, they are a very important laboratory animal.

Wild rabbits abound all over the world, but it is not a good idea to try to use these as breeding stock, or, in fact, to handle them in any way, since they are carriers of several diseases dangerous to man. Chief among these is tularemia—"rabbit fever"—which is often fatal to man. This disease is introduced into the rabbit's blood by the bite of ticks and flies.

Tularemia need not be feared in domestic stock; there has never been an instance of this disease occurring in bred stock. The restriction on using wild stock need be of no concern, however, since there is always good domestic breeding stock available at reasonable cost. For meat animals, the flesh of domestic rabbits is far superior to that of the wild strains. Rabbit meat is not seasonal, either, and can be used at any time of the year. Another advantage is that domestic rabbits attain a weight of 12 pounds or more, while a wild rabbit or hare, even the much-vaunted Western jackrabbit, rarely exceeds 6 pounds in weight.

One of the most striking breeds of rabbits is the Himalayan. These are pure-white animals with black feet, a black nose, and black ears. The constrast makes a very beautiful creature.

Rabbits are not particularly clean animals, and their hutches should be constructed with easy maintenance in mind. Particularly important is the cleaning of the floors, since rabbits pass fecal pellets in great abundance. A floor 2½ x 4 feet is needed for a doe and her litter. The height can be around 2 feet. Like hamsters, rabbits will gnaw through wooden frames, so the wire covering the cage should be on the inside. The hutch frames can be made of angle iron, although this makes them rather expensive unless you intend rearing the animals in large quantities. One-inch-mesh chicken wire is good for the floors and sides of the hutches, but you should be sure to get the kind that has the web soldered. This is far more substantial than the plain twisted wire. If you are breeding one of the very large species of meat-yielding rabbits, either install two or three braces across the bottom on which the wire floor can rest, or make the floor of ½-inch-mesh or ¾-inch-mesh hardware cloth, which is more rigid than chicken wire.

116

If the hutches are built in single tiers, heavy screening can be used for the floors, permitting the feces and urine to fall through to the ground below. This minimizes cleaning chores considerably. If, however, you build the hutches in multiple tiers of two or more stories, the floors, still of screening, should have solid sliding floors beneath them to keep the waste products from falling into the hutches below, and on their occupants. The sliding trays can be pulled out for emptying and washing, then replaced, with little trouble, and this should be done daily. A layer of cat litter spread in the cleanout trays will help keep down the odors, especially in summer, and make the trays easier to clean.

Clean hay should be used in the hutches for nesting material, and each hutch should have a nesting box or manger, about 12 x 16 inches in area and 8 inches high, with an entry hole 6 inches square at the top corner of one side. This is filled to a depth of 4 or 6 inches with clean hay. The female rabbit will pull fur from her abdomen to line the nesting cavity.

The tops of all hutches should be solid, and sloped toward the rear to shed rain. This will permit free circulation of air for the animals, yet shelter them from the direct rays of the sun. During the winter, wooden sides may be fastened in place on the rear wall and the ends, to afford protection from the cold.

Feeding rabbits is easy. Commercial rabbit pellets form the staple diet, which you may augment with all kinds of green vegetables, carrots, grasses and weeds (especially clover, dandelions, hay, and plantain), apple or pear, and potatoes. Salt blocks should be kept in each hutch.

One big problem in rearing rabbits as fur or pet animals is overfeeding. This is not the case when raising meat animals, because you want as much growth on these as possible, but for other kinds of rabbits, overfeeding makes them fat and lazy, and they breed less freely and less frequently as a result. Obesity also places a strain on their vascular systems, and probably shortens their useful lives somewhat, the same as it does in humans. It is better to feed a measured quantity of food daily. You will soon be able to judge the amount the rabbits will consume, then feed them only this amount, or even a slightly smaller quantity. Being a little hungry each day will do no harm to the animal.

Rabbits do require a constant supply of fresh clean water. This is supplied in water bottles with gravity tubes—never in dishes, since the animal will quickly foul water in a dish. You should make sure that the water bottle always has an adequate supply in it, and that the tube is working. The bottle should be suspended on the outside of the hutch, the tube reaching inside. In this way, the heavy animal cannot dislodge the bottle or knock it about.

In starting your rabbit farm it is wise to be as selective in your breeding stock as you possibly can. There are several very large establishments in the country which sell stock as breeders, and guarantee their stock. While you may pay several times as much for a pair or trio of guaranteed breeders than you will for a trio of "just rabbits" from the pet store or casual raiser, it will pay in the long run in increased output of the females, better health, size, and growth. Also, if you intend selling to laboratories, you must be able to identify the stock from which your rabbits come.

Contrary to a deeply entrenched popular belief, one should never pick up a rabbit by its ears. This can seriously injure the animal, especially if it begins to struggle or kick in your grasp. The same is true of holding the creature by the legs. Legs have been dislocated and actually broken by this method of handling. A young animal can be picked up by grasping it by the loins, just in front of the rear legs. Hold the animal firmly, but gently, and you will not bruise it. Larger species and older rabbits may be picked up by the fold of skin over the shoulders. Gather this firmly in your hand, and place your other hand under the rump of the animal to take up the weight.

The gestation period for rabbits is from thirty to thirty-two days. Does are ready to be bred at from six months to one year, depending on the breed. The small breeds are

118

ready at six months, while the giants such as the Flemish should be held until they are a year old. The young are weaned in about two months, at which time they should be salable as fryers if you have meat stock. The does can be bred four times a year, and the season makes no difference, although fertility will be highest in the spring, which is their normal mating time.

Does and bucks should not be kept together except when mating is to take place. Then the doe is introduced to the buck and left with him for a short time. Usually he will mount the female as soon as they are placed together. One mating is enough, and the doe should then be put back in her own pen. If you are not certain that a mating has taken place, the doe may again be offered to the buck after about one week. If she does not tolerate his attention, the chances are that she was mated successfully, and she may then be returned to her pen for delivery in a month. The usual litter is from six to ten. If you are breeding for vigorous stock, you may reduce the number in the litter to eight as soon as she has completed her delivery. If you have several does delivering young at nearly the same time, and some of them have smaller litters, you may place the surplus from one litter with another doe. Otherwise, you would have to destroy the surplus young.

CHAPTER 20
Minks

Fur-bearing animals have always been very popular, but not very many of them are easy to raise in captivity. There have always been rabbits, of course, and in recent years, minks and chinchillas. Chinchillas require much special treatment, but minks are simpler, and mink raising has become big business.

In the wild, minks range throughout the entire North American continent. They feed mainly on rodents such as rats and mice, fish, birds, and reptiles. Sometimes they are a serious menace to poultry farmers, although unlike several other predators, minks do not kill wantonly.

Minks are about 2 feet long when fully grown, and their fur is one of the most valuable; a good pelt is worth about $25. The color in domestic minks varies from a rich dark brown to pale tan and black. Wild minks are very dark brown to black. Minks raised in captivity have other colors. About half the mink pelts used by furriers are reared, and the other half are wild-trapped animals.

A mink. They are fierce little animals and must be handled carefully.

The gestation period varies from about forty to forty-four days, and the young are weaned in from six to eight weeks. They are born blind, and it is from three to five weeks before they open their eyes. The mating season is early in the year, from February to March. A mink has one litter per year, of from three to eight young. The usual slaughtering time is in the fall.

In captivity, mink are fed a ground-up mixture of foods rather than whole foods. This mixture is composed of animal by-products and other nutrients. They have voracious appetites; each mink eats more than its own weight each day. When a large mink farm is established, the food must be obtained in huge quantities.

Cages for rearing mink are made of heavy steel mesh and are about 16 x 30 inches in area and 12 inches high. At one end is a wooden box for the female to use as a nesting and rearing place. Water pans are secured to the other end on the outside, the screen being cut away enough

121

THIS BUILDING WAS FORMERLY THE COMMUNITY SCHOOL HOUSE, IT IS NOW BEING USED TO PACK & MIX FOOD FOR A HERD OF 15000 MINK, THE MINK HERD REQUIRES 5 TONS OF FOOD DAILY. MINK FOOD IS FED RAW & MUST BE FRESH & WHOLESOME, FOR AN OPERATION OF THIS SIZE, IT IS NECESSARY TO HAVE 200 TONS OF FOOD IN RESERVE. MINK FOOD CONSISTS OF DUCK HEADS, HORSE MEAT, CHICKEN NECKS & BACKS, COTTAGE CHEESE BEEF BYPRODUCTS AND A SPECIALLY PREPARED COOKED WHOLE GRAIN CEREAL.

THE ABOVE INGREDIENTS ARE GROUND THRU A 50 HP. GRINDER & MIXED WITH VITAMINS AND MINERALS RESULTING IN HEALTHY MINK WITH SUPERIOR QUALITY FUR.

VISIT OUR FUR SHOP
ACROSS THE STREET

Ralph & Fred Space
OWNERS

This sign at Space Farms, a large mink farm in New Jersey, makes clear the problems involved in feeding the voracious animals.

Below and opposite: Rows of mink sheds at Space Farms and the interior of one of them. If all the mink cages at the farm were placed end to end, they would stretch 5 miles.

to permit the animals to reach the water, but not so much as to permit their escape. The cages are fastened together in rows of eighteen, and these rows are set on stands. A typical mink house is an open shed 300 feet long and about 20 feet wide, with a low roof of corrugated sheet metal. The interior accommodates two rows of cages with a wide center aisle. A steel platform is fastened inside each cage at one side of the front end, and the water dish is at the other end. In feeding the animals, a cart holding a large tank filled with the mushy mixed food is driven down the aisle, and the attendant dips a ladle of food and throws it through the screen of the cage onto the platform. The mink soon clean it up from there.

In the summer, these low-roofed mink houses are unbelievably hot, and in winter they are very cold, but the mink seem to tolerate the climate with no difficulty. Since the sheds are open on all sides there is air circulation. The cages are all screen, and so droppings fall through to the ground beneath, where they pile up and are easy to remove at intervals.

A well-run mink ranch will carry 20,000 minks or even more at all times. This represents an enormous value in the pelts, and every precaution is taken to ensure the health and safety of the animals.

A cleaned inside-out mink skin being stretched on a drying board. Once they are tanned the pelts are worth about $25 each.

Breeders are always available from the better ranches. Good animals command very high prices, up to many hundreds of dollars per pair in some cases. To start a mink ranch, you would need several pairs, and they should be from different bloodlines to avoid too much inbreeding.

Accurate and complete records are kept of all matings and births and of the disposition of all animals. Mating

124

times and other pertinent data are recorded on weather-proof cards that are attached to each cage. At any time the mink rancher can tell just which female delivered what litter, how many young, when they were delivered, when they are due for skinning, and all other information. Selected animals are not skinned but retained as breeders. They are carefully segregated to maintain different bloodlines and are mated for color, size, luxuriance of fur, etc.

Before you begin to market the pelts you should build up your breeding stock. When you have a large enough stable of breeders to produce a good number of young each season, then you can start taking pelts for sale. You should always put back several new breeding pairs each season to add to the starters, in order to keep your stock at a high level.

Cages can be added as your expanding farm requires them, but from the start the sheds should be large enough to accommodate long rows of cages. Otherwise you will find yourself up against a real maintenance problem, running from one small shed to another to care for the animals. This results in too much inefficiency to make the venture profitable.

There is, of course, no point in raising minks unless you are willing to skin them yourself, for there is no market for unskinned carcasses or for live animals except as breeders. The skinning of small animals is an art in itself and is somewhat beyond the scope of this book; the best way to learn how it is done is to go to a mink farm during the skinning season—usually late November and December— and ask to be allowed to watch the process. The animals are killed painlessly either by breaking their necks or by gassing them with carbon monoxide or some other gas. After the proper cuts have been made, the skin is peeled off the animal inside out, starting at the rear and taking great care to keep blood and fat from touching the fur. The skin is scraped to remove all flesh and then dried on a special board. Most mink farms then send the skins elsewhere for tanning.

CHAPTER 21
Flying Squirrels

Flying squirrels are the most endearing of all small wild animals. They have cute faces with a Disneylike expression, are friendly and trusting, and are no great trouble to keep. Unfortunately, they are completely nocturnal, and are seldom out when you want them to be. That is why flying squirrels, even though they are our commonest animals, are practically never seen in the wild. Also they are generally in the treetops rather than on the ground.

Flying squirrels have no commercial value at all, but they do make excellent pets and can be sold in small quantities to pet stores.

Flying squirrels actually do not fly—they glide. Their ability to glide from tree to tree is little short of amazing. They can cover 150 feet with ease, from the top of one tree to the middle or lower branches of another. The gliding ability is made possible by folds of skin along the sides, extending from the front to the rear legs. When the animal extends its legs, these folds open out like a parachute, cupping the air beneath them and forming a planing surface.

Cages for these animals must be high and must have some kind of branch inside from which the little creatures

126

A flying squirrel on top of its log house. This one was born in captivity and was five years old at the time of the photograph.

may launch themselves in exercising, which they do for hours on end at night. There must also be some kind of shelter that is adequate for both winter and summer. A section of log about 2 feet long and not less than 10 or 12 inches in diameter makes an ideal shelter if it is hollowed out to a depth of 6 to 8 inches, with a 2-inch hole at the top of the hollow. A second section of the log, left solid, about 8 inches thick, is laid on top of the hollowed section, making a roof and affording insulation by its thickness. The squirrels will chew the hole to suit themselves.

Food for flying squirrels is varied. They subsist almost entirely on fruits and nuts in the wild. They also search eagerly for large insects. Grasshoppers, crickets, and similar insects are an important part of their diet; if they suffer from protein deficiency, cannibalism is likely to develop. Water may be supplied in a dropper bottle, hung on the outside of the cage with the tube projecting inside. Since the squirrels run about the inside walls of their cage as if they were broad highways, it really does not matter where you put the feeding and watering devices. The animals will be able to reach them with no difficulty.

Breeding stock of these animals can be purchased at about $25 per pair, or you can trap wild stock to start. After you have located flying squirrels, trapping them is rather easy. These animals nest in holes in trees, and very often take over the nesting places of other creatures, notably screech owls and sparrow hawks. Boxes erected for these birds house a family of flying squirrels nearly as often as they do the animals for which they were intended. Boxes about 10 inches square and 12 inches deep can be fastened in trees from 15 to 25 feet off the ground, and watched carefully to see if the squirrels occupy them. If you knock on the tree trunk the squirrel, if there is one in the box, will pop out and scamper away. The next day you can trap it.

A tube of metal fly screening is made, about a foot long and 4 inches in diameter. Sew or wire the edges together to form the tube, then fold one end flat to close it. Now, with the help of an assistant, if you cannot perform both operations alone, hold the open end of the tube against the hole in which the squirrel is nesting, and rap the tree sharply. The squirrel will pop out of the hole into the tube, and you instantly squash the end shut to confine it. It is as easy as that.

If you time your trapping activities correctly, you may get a pregnant female that will deliver her litter after you have her at home. Flying squirrels mate in the winter, and the first litter of young are born in March and April. If you trap adult squirrels, always examine the nesting hole carefully to make certain you do not leave a litter of babies there. If they are young, they can be taken too, and the entire family transferred to your cage at home. The mother will continue to rear the young, even after the transfer. From two to six babies are delivered in a litter, and the female will have two or three litters each year. The young are born blind, and they are weaned in about ten weeks. They live up to ten years, a very long lifespan for such a tiny creature.

PART V
BIRDS

CHAPTER 22
Poultry

Poultry is raised for one of two reasons—eggs or meat. Keeping chickens is no great problem if you live in the country or on a farm. Meat chickens may be permitted to run freely, since you are not concerned with finding the eggs but only with getting heavy growth of meat on the bird. Even free chickens, however, need auxiliary food supplies. They also need shelter of some kind, especially in the country, where night predators may wreak havoc with a flock of chickens. Opossums, raccoons, weasels, minks, foxes, and many other animals eat chickens, and so do large owls at night and large hawks during the day.

Chickens have been bred into many different bloodlines for many different purposes. Egg layers are usually unfit for meat production, since their bodies are small and thin, and the meat is sparsely distributed over the carcass. Meat producers, on the other hand, are stocky, fatter birds, all their energy going to the fleshing-out process, and they are not spectacular producers of eggs. Then there are intermediate breeds which are useful for both egg and meat production, but are not superior in either area.

Some of the breeds good for meat are the Rhode Island

Bantams are raised not for meat or eggs but for show stock or to serve as foster mothers for game-bird eggs.

Red, the Plymouth Rock, the Barred Rocks, and the Wyandotte. The best laying breeds are the White Leghorn, of course, and the Black Minorca. Few people are aware that the Black Minorca is an even better egg producer than the Leghorn—better both because of the size of the eggs, which are snow-white and nearly as large as duck eggs, and because of the regularity with which the hens lay. The Minorca is a larger breed than the Leghorn. Both Minorcas and Leghorns fly with ease, and they must be kept in covered runs or they will disperse all over the land.

If you are interested in egg production, then you need have no males in the flock. The hens will lay as readily when their eggs are infertile as they do after being serviced by a rooster. Egg flocks should be confined in runs, with a house at one end inside of which you may install nesting boxes. These can be batteries of commercial metal nests, or just divided spaces made of boards. A thick layer of hay should be put into each nesting space, which the hen will distribute to suit herself. At first, the hens may not accept the nests and will lay their eggs on the floor of the house or even out in the run. They can be induced to accept their

131

nests by placing a "nest egg" in each nest. These are painted wooden eggs, or ceramic ones, and the idea is that the hen, seeing one egg in the nest already, will lay hers in with it, building up a clutch on which to set. After the hens have begun to lay in the nests, the nest egg is no longer needed and may be removed.

There are a great many odd traditions in poultry raising. One practice, designed so the chickens can be allowed to run free during the day, is to build the house and nesting area, rub the roosts, the door, and the run leading into the house with bacon fat, then confine the hens within it for a week. After a week the chickens are released, and they will thereafter run all day, foraging for themselves, and return at dusk to the house and enter it without having to be driven inside. Just what the bacon fat is supposed to do is unknown to me. The effect would certainly repel a human being, especially after a week in the hot sun. However, my father would never have thought of establishing a new hen house without this treatment, although he could never explain the reason to me.

Runs for chickens should be about 10 feet wide and as long as you have space, not less than 20 feet, not counting the space needed for the house on the end. This should be the width of the run and about 6 to 8 feet deep. Make the house high enough so you can stand erect inside; otherwise cleaning, gathering eggs, rearranging nesting material, and painting will be difficult. The floor of the henhouse should be raised from the ground not less than 8 inches. Even better is a concrete floor, and, if you intend any continuous rearing of poultry, you should consider concrete seriously. A concrete floor can be hosed down, scraped, and swept easily, and maintenance is practically nil. If the floor is of wood, it should be supported on floor beams made of 2x10 lumber, spaced 16 inches on centers. The floor itself may be made of tongue-and-groove lumber, which is strong but has cracks that can harbor mites and lice, or of plywood, in which case plyscored exterior panels not less than $\frac{5}{8}$ inch thick should be used.

The support for the house may be four or six columns of concrete blocks, set into the ground on footings of concrete about 2 feet deep and 24 inches square. The blocks may either be mortared together or laid up dry. Mortaring is, naturally, far stronger, and if you live in an area subject to high winds during the winter you should mortar the blocks. Two blocks above ground makes a good height to raise the house, and the sides can be screened with the same chicken wire used to enclose the runs. The side of the house facing the run should be left free of screen to open it to the run, but it should be closed off with removable boards until the hens have established their nesting habits. As soon as they have accepted their nests and lay in them, these boards may be removed, and the birds permitted to go under the house. This will afford a shade area during the heat of the day, and some protection from the elements when they are ranging in the yards.

The sides and end of the yards should be protected from digging predators in some way. The best way is to dig a trench, outlining the entire run, install fence posts in the trench at the proper intervals, and fasten netting to the posts from the bottoms of the trenches, then fill the trenches with soil well packed down. The trenches should be not less than 18 inches deep, to discourage animals from digging down under the screening.

Hen houses should be disinfected regularly by washing them down with a half-and-half mixture of anthracene oil and kerosene. This may either be applied with a brush or sprayed, on the walls, roosts and floor. The floor should be covered with 2 or 3 inches of hay or straw, and when this becomes soiled enough to be noticeable, it should be removed, the floor should be cleaned and sprayed, and new straw should be put down.

Chickens are subject to infestation by mites and lice. These may be seen on the undersides of the roosts. A line of nicotine sulphate placed along the roosts during the daytime, before the chickens use them, will effectively control the pests.

133

Each hen should be allowed about 4 square feet of floor space in a hen house. A house 10 feet wide and 8 feet deep would comfortably accommodate twenty hens. In a pinch, twenty-four hens could be kept in a house this size.

Ideally, chicken runs should be constructed in an L shape, with the henhouse at the juncture of the L. Each leg of the run should be the same size, and the house should have a door leading to each leg, each door capable of being closed off. The soil should be tilled and grain seed sown in the yards. Wheat, rye, oats, or just grass is fine. The chickens should be permitted to use one run, the other side being permitted to grow. When the first run has been eaten off, the door to it can be closed and the other door opened to the new run. The old run can be resown to sprout fresh fodder.

The netting used for chicken runs can be ordinary poultry wire. It is best to close the top of each run wtih the same netting at the beginning, even though you are intending to keep chickens that normally do not fly. The runs should be made high enough, if they are covered, to permit you to walk upright, or at the very least, just slightly stooped. The soil inside each run should be limed at least once a year, using agricultural lime available at feed stores. This will help keep down mites and fleas and sweeten the soil, at the same time providing lime for the growing grain or grass.

If you live in a part of the country that has a large population of predatory owls, it would be good insurance to make a double roof for the run, about 4 inches apart. This can easily be accomplished by making the top rails of the run out of 4x4 lumber and tacking the screening to both the top and the bottom of the rails. The reason for the double ceiling is that owls will swoop down at the runs, frightening the birds until they fly frantically to escape the predator. Since their instinct is to fly up, they do this, sticking their heads out through the holes in the screen, and the owls snip off the heads as fast as they appear. The double netting prevents this from happening.

The feeding of poultry has become so organized that

there is nothing really to discuss in the way of special foods. Commercial feed stores sell everything needed for chickens in packages—baby chick scratch, cracked grains, growing mash, egg-laying mash, and individual grains such as corn, wheat, and oats. The mashes form a complete diet for most purposes, augmented, perhaps, with a little crushed oyster shell for extra calcium and grits. Mash should be fed to the chickens in hopper feeders, kept filled. Grains can be scattered on the ground once daily, a handful or two per chicken being all that is needed. This will permit the chickens to scratch for their feed, giving them needed exercise with the nourishment.

In winter, it helps to mix the mash with hot water, making a warm, wet mixture. The chickens seem to relish the hot food during very cold weather. Make the mash damp enough to form a paste, but not soupy wet. This is not, of course, fed in hoppers, as the wet mixture would not feed through the chute. Place it in a shallow pan, and remove the pan when the food has been consumed.

Bantams are very popular among poultry fanciers. Many of the bantam breeds are diminutive specimens of standard breeds, looking exactly like their larger cousins only in miniature. Many other bantam breeds have been artificially created over many years of selective breeding, and have no counterpart in the large species.

Usually, bantams are raised where space for poultry is limited. However, they are not practical either for meat production or for egg production; the eggs are very small—even smaller than pullet eggs. Most bantams are reared as show stock or as pets. Some of the breeds, especially the Cochin, become as tame as kittens, following their owners about and even sitting in their laps.

The Japanese have been breeding special strains of bantams for centuries, and have produced some really unusual types of birds. The Silkie, for example, has feathers more like fur, and black skin. The Black-tailed Jap has tail feathers as long as 10 feet. These birds must have tall posts on which to roost, so their tails can hang naturally, not catching on things or dragging in the dirt. The curious-looking top-knotted Polish bantams are popular birds, as are the trim Golden or Silver Seabrights and the Cornish Game Bantams. These last are short, heavy birds, wide legged and stocky. A constant favorite is the Cochin. This friendly little bantam has feathered legs and feet and is a fat, round ball of fluff. The Black Cochin has a wonderful iridescent sheen on the feathers, making it very beautiful when it moves about in the sunlight.

Bantam hens are used a great deal by game-bird fanciers to hatch the game-bird eggs. Many wild or game birds will not set in captivity, and regular chickens are so heavy that they crack the fragile eggs. Bantams take readily to setting a clutch of wild eggs, and a Cochin can cover a clutch of fifteen eggs with no difficulty. The hatch under bantams is better than incubator hatchings, and much easier to manage if you have no incubator of your own, but are forced to farm out the work.

In rearing bantams, especially as show stock, you should take time and trouble to look for absolutely top-quality stock. Many hatcheries dealing with fancy breeds of poultry have pedigreed stock, at premium prices, in the form of hatching eggs, baby chicks, or adults. It is well worth the price to get fine breeder stock if you are going after show awards with your birds.

Bantams bred for show should not be permitted to run on the ground. Their yards should have a wire netting floor, raised about 8 inches above ground. This can be made of 1-inch-mesh poultry netting, stretched tightly between the walls of the run. The birds can be kept indoors in large houses, too, but their diet should then be augmented by the addition of codliver oil in the mash or on the grain to supply needed vitamins.

CHAPTER 23

Game Birds

For many decades, bird fanciers have been raising wild game birds for pleasure and for showing at exhibits. Recently, however, the raising of some of these birds has been increasing by leaps and bounds as a means of stocking shooting preserves. Since the first years of this century there has been a decline in certain game birds, because of over-kill, the disappearance of breeding grounds, and other factors. Some owners of large tracts of wooded and field land began importing game birds to release them on their property to afford hunting sport for themselves and their friends. The bird most commonly imported was the common ring-necked pheasant. Soon these birds were being reared in large numbers, and finally the rearing of pheasants for game-preserve stocking became a big business.

From being private shooting grounds, many of the large tracts have been turned into fee-paid shooting preserves, where a hunter can go, and, by paying a fee, hunt the place for game birds. These places either rear their own pheasants in quantities or buy them from people who raise them for the purpose, delivering a regular number of birds each season on a continuing purchase plan.

Game birds should never be reared on ground that has accommodated domestic fowl. Pheasants and quail, particularly, are extremely susceptible to diseases of chickens, ducks, and geese, and even though the domestic birds may not have been ill with a disease, the wild birds could become infected. Anything used in the keeping of domestic birds must be thoroughly sterilized before using it for the wild species. It is even better to discard all apparatus and start with new. The ground itself must be sterilized, turned over deeply, and permitted a rest period over a full season before running wild game birds on it.

Pheasant eggs are sold by large poultry breeders, for hatching yourself, in lots of 25, 50, and 100. They are hatched under bantam chickens or in incubators. The chicks are almost immediately self-sufficient, running about and feeding on baby chick scratch feed. Their growth is rapid. However, pens devoted to the raising of chicks, called brooder pens, are most desirable, and, if you intend to rear any quantity of birds, these pens are a necessity, since the growing chicks should not be kept with adult birds.

Commercial feeds and pellets are available for game birds, so you need not take the time and trouble to mix your own feed rations.

The first thing you must do before beginning to raise any game bird is to investigate your state regulations regarding the possession of such animals. Nearly every state in the union requires that you take out a license for rearing, buying, selling, and keeping any game bird. Some states are more restrictive than others. You risk much trouble and a possible fine if you do not comply with whatever regulations your state enforces. A letter to the conservation department of your state will bring you all the information on the bird you wish to raise.

Whenever possible, it is advisable to keep your rearing

A ring-necked pheasant in a run.

operation small enough to enable you to hatch out your eggs under bantams. True, this necessitates keeping a battery of bantam hens at all times, and limits the hatching operations to the times the bantams want to set, but the resulting hatches are worth it in higher percentage of hatching, healthier chicks, and better control of the eggs, during the time of incubation. Eggs hatched in mechanical incubators must be tended constantly. The temperature and humidity must be kept constant, and circulation of air is a necessity. The eggs are stacked on their sides, or small end down to permit the gases forming inside as the embryo develops to find their way into the chamber at the top of the large end of the shell. The eggs must be turned 45 degrees from three to five times daily, up to the twenty-first day, after which they need not be turned any more. The turning is to prevent the developing chick from growing to the shell. Seven days after beginning the incubation, the eggs should be candled to determine which are infertile. These should be discarded. Fourteen days after the start of incubation, the eggs are again candled. This time is it to determine which contain living and developing embryos. Those with dead embryos should be removed and discarded at this time. An infertile egg, or one that has died in the developing stages, will generate gases that can kill all the other eggs in the tray unless removed.

Candling is a simple process. You merely hold the egg up to a strong light, with all the extraneous light obstructed, and look through it. You will plainly see the embryo inside, and you can, by watching it for a moment, determine if it is alive or not. To obstruct the extraneous light, cut a small hole, just under the size of the egg, in a piece of cardboard, and place a flashlight or other light behind it. The egg is held against the hole to candle it.

One very important thing to remember in incubating any eggs is to keep accurate and complete records. It is not enough to put the eggs in the machine, then after a few weeks say, "Well, they should be hatching tomorrow or the next day." Tomorrow or the next day is not good enough, because the loss of the entire hatching can take place between tomorrow and the next day if the chicks are not attended to. When a tray begins to hatch, wait until all the eggs hatch before opening the incubator to remove the chicks. You may very well kill the remaining eggs if the incubator is opened one or more times to remove a few chicks.

The incubation periods for some of the game birds are:
Ring-necked pheasants—23 to 24 days at 100 degrees
Grouse—23 days at 101 degrees
Quail (bobwhite)—23 days at 101 degrees
Partridges—22 to 23 days at 101 degrees
Reeves and Lady Amherst pheasants incubate in the same period as the ring-necked species, but Silver pheasant take twenty-six days at the same temperature to hatch.

The chicks are left in the incubator for from twenty-four to thirty-six hours, then they are tranferred to the brooders.

140

These should be put in operation the day before the chicks are placed in them, to make sure the temperature is even and holding at the proper level. A wire netting fence about a foot high can surround each brooder to contain the chicks; several watering founts and feed pans are placed inside the fence. Not less than 72 square inches of floor space should be allowed each chick in the brooder.

Brooders must be kept in closed areas to prevent the chicks from escaping. They are very active, and can soon shift for themselves, and you may lose a brood if it is not contained securely. Outdoor runs must be screened on the top as well as the sides and ends, and it is very important to make the top a double screen if you live in a wooded area. The owls will consider the birds legitimate prey, be-heading a flock in a night. Actually, if it were not for the loss of the birds, it is interesting to watch the owls at work. They glide down to the top of the run on silent wings, alighting

A peacock, sometimes reared for show.

with scarcely a tremor on the wire. They wait until several birds are in the open, then suddenly spread their wings wide and hoot. The game birds are thrown into immediate terror, thrashing wildly about and trying to fly out of danger. Their instinct being to fly up, they bang against the top screen. Holding themselves there by a frantic thrashing of wings, they poke their heads and necks through the mesh, and the owl dines on game-bird head, the decapitated body falling to the ground inside the run where the owl cannot reach it.

Water is supplied in fountain-type bottles, which have a pan that screws onto the jar and fills with water when the jar is inverted. It is better to use several small jars—about quart size—rather than one large one. This way the water can be distributed at several places under the brooder or in the run, and the birds will be more apt to find it. Also, the small jars are easier to clean and fill than the large ones. The water should be replenished each day, and the fount thoroughly cleaned each time. Water founts should be raised slightly so the pans do not get fouled with droppings or litter. Any fount that has been fouled with droppings should be cleaned and refilled as soon as it is noticed. A good system is to employ one water fount and one 12-inch feed hopper for every fifteen pheasant chicks, or the same for each fifteen partridge, or for each thirty-six quail chicks.

Besides quail and pheasants, partridges are very popular among game birds. The common partridge is not so much in favor as the chukar partridge. This last is not indigenous to the United States; it was imported from India. Another favorite is the Hungarian partridge, but the chukar takes the lead in numbers produced.

Bantams are used to hatch partridge eggs, since it is difficult to get the hens to set in captivity. However, often escaped hens will remain in the vicinity from which they escaped, and they can be found setting clutches of eggs under bushes, or even in old abandoned shacks or packing cases. Chukars are handsome birds, nearly alike in the sexes. The way to tell them apart is to look at the backs of

142

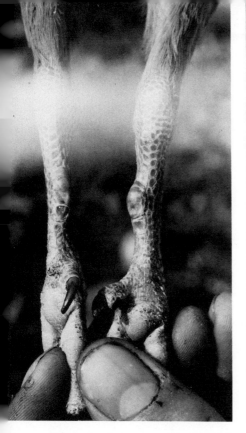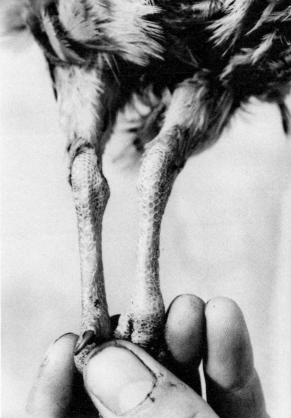

The male chukar partridge has a horny swelling on the leg just above the foot. The female, otherwise hard to distinguish from the male, has no swelling.

the legs. The males have a large horny growth on the back legs, and this growth is considerably less prominent on the females. The growth corresponds to the spur in other birds.

Both species of partridges are reared much the same way as quail, with the same feeding requirements. They eat commercial game-bird pellets, insects, worms, and any wild seed found in their run. Growing mash is also available commercially. The same precaution about not using land run over by domestic fowl must be taken for these partridges, and the same types of runs and housing is needed. The amount of space is necessarily larger than for quail, but a run large enough to accommodate pheasant is fine for chukar or Hungarian partridge.

In order to rear partridge successfully, it is necessary to

Chukar partridges. The bird on the eggs is a female, the other is a male.

keep them from the ground. This means raised wire netting floors in the runs and the houses. The netting should be raised about 2 feet off the ground, and stretched tightly enough to support the weight of the covey of birds without sagging. One-inch-mesh chicken wire is fine for the floor, although ½-inch-mesh or ¾-inch-mesh hardware cloth would be better. The birds are less apt to catch their feet in the hardware cloth. Grouse, especially the wonderful ruffed grouse, are impossible to rear unless you use a wire floor, and even then are very difficult to bring to maturity. One might better stick to rearing pheasant, quail, and partridge. A pair of adult breeders of ruffed grouse may cost as much as $150 or $200, and then there is no guarantee that you will be successful in rearing them.

CHAPTER 24
Disinfection for Poultry and Game Birds

In rearing chickens, bantams, or any domestic poultry, as well as in rearing game birds such as quail, pheasant, and partridge, cleanliness in the pens, runs, and houses is a real necessity. Epidemic sicknesses can run through an entire flock of birds in a very short time. Once such a disease has attacked, the area may be infectious for a considerable time after the birds have died and been removed.

Besides infestation by mites, ticks, fleas, and lice, there are several virus diseases common to poultry, and respiratory ailments such as pneumonia are also common.

Powders are available for dusting the bodies of the birds to eliminate parasitic pests, and these should be used with caution and strictly in accordance with the instructions on the labels. Usually they are not for use on or near baby chicks.

After the birds have been treated, there remains the problem of clearing the nesting, roosting, and sleeping areas from the parasites. This can best be done with any of several oil-type sprays sold for the purpose. Kerosene is also effective in killing parasitic insects, and so is creosote. The birds should be removed from the area being treated, and should not be returned to it until every part is completely dry. Returning birds too quickly to a house or pen treated with creosote will quickly kill them. Besides being thoroughly dry, creosoted areas must be thoroughly aired out before use.

146

A strong solution of lye is very effective as a sterilizer. It can be sprayed or applied with a long-handled brush. Remember that a strong lye solution can burn your skin very severely on contact.

No disinfectant is effective unless all droppings and litter have been removed. The floors and roosts, nest boxes, walls, and any other fixed piece of apparatus should be scraped clean and then brushed off before applying the disinfectant. Feeding and watering devices should be removed before the disinfectant is applied. These can be cleaned and sterilized separately.

All new birds introduced to your rearing quarters should be quarantined for at least two weeks before they are mixed in with the existing birds. During this quarantine, the birds should be carefully inspected for parasites, and treated for them if they are found to be present. This is especially true of bantam hens being used for incubating game bird eggs. They should be thoroughly examined and cleaned of parasites before permitting them to enter or run on the area used for nesting. It is far easier to eliminate the parasite pests from a bird's body than from an entire nesting area.

Rarely is a wild bird found to be free of parasites. While domestically raised birds are not so infected, still you should exercise all caution when they are first obtained. Reputable breeders who sell stock for breeding usually have taken whatever precautions they could to see that their birds are parasite-free. Even then, there is a chance that your birds will arrive with visitors in the feathers.

Treatments for different diseases are available, and are usually given to the birds in their drinking water. Follow directions accompanying each remedy carefully.

In addition to diseases and parasites, the game-bird breeder has to contend with predators, if he lives in a rural area. There are several predators that consider poultry and game birds their natural prey and will make considerable inroads in a flock if not curtailed. Unfortunately, sometimes the killing of predators to protect one's business of rearing birds conflicts with state laws and regulations, since many predators are also valuable fur-bearing animals and are rigidly protected by law. It is very possible that the states will permit casual trapping of predatory animals in the case of game-bird farms. This seems logical, because most states require the game-bird raiser to have a license, and certainly should not hamper the execution of that license by curtailing the activity for which it was issued. However, it is good policy, when applying for the bird license, to inquire also about safeguards against predators.

The runs should be made with predation in mind, in any case, and the sides and ends of the wire set in trenches. One good way to discourage digging under the runs is to put 3-foot-wide poultry netting in the trench, for a depth of a foot or so, bending the wire above ground at right angles to the trench, facing out away from the run to lie flat on the ground. It can be held in position with a few stakes if necessary. The sides of the run are then placed in the trench also, and the trench filled with dirt and tamped. The netting should be of 1-inch-mesh size. The wide border around the run walls will discourage animals from digging under the wire. Woodchucks may be an exception, since often they start their tunneling some distance away from where they want to end up, thus missing the protective border entirely. However, since woodchucks are rarely protected, you should have no trouble either shooting them or trapping them if they do begin to tunnel into the runs. Woodchucks themselves are not necessarily predators of poultry and game birds, but their tunnels afford a broad highway for real predators.

In states where predatory animals are protected, and if you are unable to obtain a killing permit, you have recourse to live-trapping. Several firms manufacture steel traps that take the animals alive without harming them. The Mustang Manufacturing Company of Houston, Texas, makes a full line of such traps, and these can be used to catch the predator. Then, still in the trap, the animal may be transported a considerable distance away from your area and liberated. The chance of its returning to your runs is remote.

Appendix:
Sources of
Further Information

Each state has a special department devoted to the management of its game birds and wildlife. A letter to this department will bring you information on obtaining licenses, whether or not you can deal with predators, information on feeding and housing birds and animals, and a wealth of free information you would otherwise have difficulty finding. The address of the department for each state is listed in this appendix. Also listed are the addresses of the five regional offices of the United States government, and the offices in the provinces of Canada.

149

Federal Government:
United States Department of the Interior
Bureau of Sport Fisheries and Wildlife
Washington, D.C. 20240

Alabama:
Director, Department of Conservation
64 North Union Street
Montgomery, Alabama 36104

Alaska:
Commissioner, Department of Fish and Game
Subport Building
Juneau, Alaska 99801

Arizona:
Director, Game and Fish Department
P. O. Box 9095
Phoenix, Arizona 85023

Arkansas:
Director, Game and Fish Commission
Game and Fish Building
Little Rock, Arkansas 72201

California:
Director, Department of Fish and Game
1416 Ninth Street
Sacramento, California 95814

Colorado:
Director, Department of Game, Fish and Parks
6060 Broadway
Denver, Colorado 80216

Connecticut:
Director, Board of Fisheries and Game
State Office Building
Hartford, Connecticut 06106

Delaware:
Director, Board of Game and Fish Commissioners
Box 457
Dover, Delaware 19901

District of Columbia:
Chief of Police
300 Indiana Avenue
Washington, D.C. 20001

Florida:
Director, Game and Freshwater Fish Commission
620 South Meridan
Tallahassee, Florida 32304

Georgia:
Director, Game and Fish Commission
401 State Capitol
Atlanta, Georgia 30334

Hawaii:
Director, Division of Fish and Game
Department of Land and Natural Resources
400 South Beretania Street
Honolulu, Hawaii 96813

Idaho:
Director, Fish and Game Department
600 South Walnut, Box 25
Boise, Idaho 83707

Illinois:
Director, Department of Conservation
102 State Office Building
Springfield, Illinois 62706

Indiana:
Director, Department of Natural Resources
603 State Office Building
Indianapolis, Indiana 46204

Iowa:
Director, Iowa Conservation Commission
East 7th and Court Avenue
Des Moines, Iowa 50319

Kansas:
Director, Forestry, Fish and Game Commission
P.O. Box F
Pratt, Kansas 67124

150

Kentucky:
Commissioner, Department of Fish and Wildlife Resources
State Office Building Annex
Frankfort, Kentucky 40601

Louisiana:
Director, Wildlife and Fisheries Commission
400 Royal Street
New Orleans, Louisiana 70130

Maine:
Commissioner, Department of Inland Fisheries and Game
State House
Augusta, Maine 04330

Maryland:
Director, Department of Game and Inland Fish
Box 231
Annapolis, Maryland 21404

Massachusetts:
Director, Division of Fisheries and Game
100 Cambridge Street
Boston, Massachusetts 02202

Michigan:
Director, Department of Conservation
Stevens T. Mason Building
Lansing, Michigan 48926

Minnesota:
Commissioner, Department of Conservation
301 Centennial Building
St. Paul, Minnesota 55101

Mississippi:
Executive Director, Game and Fish Commission
P.O. Box 451
Jackson, Mississippi 39205

Missouri:
Director, Department of Conservation
P.O. Box 180
Jefferson City, Missouri 65102

Montana:
Director, Fish and Game Department
Helena, Montana 59601

Nebraska:
Director, Game, Forestation, and Park Commission
State Capitol Building
Lincoln, Nebraska 68509

Nevada:
Director, Fish and Game Commission
Box 678
Reno, Nevada 89510

New Hampshire:
Director, Fish and Game Department
34 Bridge Street
Concord, New Hampshire 03301

New Jersey:
Director, Division of Fish and Game
Department of Conservation and Economic Development
Box 1390
Trenton, New Jersey 08625

New Mexico:
Director, Department of Game and Fish
State Capitol Building
Santa Fe, New Mexico 87501

New York:
Director, Fish and Game, Conservation Department
State Office Buildings, Campus
Albany, New York 12226

North Carolina:
Executive Director, Wildlife Resources Commission
P.O. Box 2919
Raleigh, North Carolina 27602

North Dakota:
Commissioner, Game and Fish Department
103½ South 3rd. Street
Bismarck, North Dakota 58501

Ohio:
Department of Natural Resources
1106 Ohio Departments Building
Columbus, Ohio 43215

Oklahoma:
Director, Department of Wildlife
 Conservation
P.O. Box 53465
Oklahoma City, Oklahoma 73105

Oregon:
Director, State Game Commission
Box 3503
Portland, Oregon 97208

Pennsylvania:
Executive Director, Game Commis-
 sion
P.O. Box 1567
Harrisburg, Pennsylvania 17120

Rhode Island:
Chief, Division of Conservation
Department of Natural Resources
83 Park Street
Providence, Rhode Island 02903

South Carolina:
Director, Division of Game
Wildlife Resources Department
Box 167
Columbia, South Carolina 29202

South Dakota:
Director, Department of Game,
 Fish, and Parks
State Office Building
Pierre, South Dakota 57501

Tennessee:
Director, Game and Fish Commis-
 sion
Room 600, Doctor's Building
Nashville, Tennessee 37203

Texas:
Executive Director, Parks and Wild-
 life Department
John H. Reagan Building
Austin, Texas 78701

Utah:
Director, Division of Fish and
 Game, Department of Natural
 Resources
1596 West North Temple
Salt Lake City, Utah 84116

Vermont:
Commissioner, Fish and Game De-
 partment
Montpelier, Vermont 05602

Virginia:
Executive Director, Commission of
 Game and Inland Fisheries
Box 1642
Richmond, Virginia 23213

Washington:
Director, Department of Game
600 North Capitol Way
Olympia, Washington 98501

West Virginia:
Chief, Fish and Game Division
Department of Natural Resources
State Office Building, 3
Charleston, West Virginia 25305

Wisconsin:
Conservation Administrator, Divi-
 sion of Conservation
Department of Natural Resources
Box 450
Madison, Wisconsin 53701

Wyoming:
Commissioner, Game and Fish
 Commission
P.O. Box 1589
Cheyenne, Wyoming 82001

These are the regional directors of the United States and each director covers a number of states.

Region One (Alaska, California, Hawaii, Idaho, Montana, Nevada, Oregon and Washington):

Regional Director, Bureau of Sport Fisheries and Wildlife
U.S. Department of the Interior
730 NE Pacific Street, P.O. Box 3737
Portland, Oregon 97208

Region Two (Arizona, Colorado, Kansas, New Mexico, Oklahoma, Texas, Utah, and Wyoming):

Regional Director, Bureau of Sport Fisheries and Wildlife
U.S. Department of the Interior
Federal Building, P.O. Box 1306
517 Gold Avenue, Southwest
Albuquerque, New Mexico 87103

Region Three (Illinois, Indiana, Iowa, Michigan, Minnesota, Missouri, Nebraska, Ohio, North and South Dakota, and Wisconsin):

Regional Director, Bureau of Sport Fisheries and Wildlife
U.S. Department of the Interior
Federal Building, Fort Snelling
Twin Cities, Minnesota 55111

Region Four (Alabama, Arkansas, Florida, Georgia, Kentucky, Louisiana, Maryland, Mississippi, North and South Carolina, Tennessee, Virginia, and District of Columbia):

Regional Director, Bureau of Sport Fisheries and Wildlife
U.S. Department of the Interior
Peachtree-Seventh Building
Atlanta, Georgia 30323

Region Five (Connecticut, Delaware, Maine, Massachusetts, New Hampshire, New Jersey, New York, Pennsylvania, Rhode Island, Vermont, and West Virginia):

Regional Director, Bureau of Sport Fisheries and Wildlife
U.S. Department of the Interior
U.S. Post Office and Courthouse
Boston, Massachusetts 02109

Canadian Government:
Chief, Canadian Wildlife Service
Ottawa, Canada

Alberta:
Fish and Wildlife Division, Department of Lands and Forests
Edmonton, Alberta, Canada

British Columbia:
Chief, Game Management
Fish and Game Bureau
Parliaments Building
Victoria, British Columbia, Canada

Manitoba:
Director of Wildlife
Department of Mines and Natural Resources
Winnipeg, Manitoba, Canada

New Brunswick:
Chief, Fish and Wildlife Bureau
Department of Lands and Mines
Fredericton, New Brunswick, Canada

Newfoundland:
Director of Wildlife
Department of Mines, Agriculture and Resources
St. Johns, Newfoundland, Canada

Northwest Territories:
Deputy Commissioner of N.W.T.
Vimy Building
Ottawa, N.W.T., Canada

Nova Scotia:
Fish and Game Association
P.O. Box 654
Halifax, Nova Scotia, Canada

Ontario:
Chief, Fish and Wildlife Bureau
Department of Lands and Forests
Parliaments Building
Toronto, Ontario, Canada

Prince Edward Island:
Director of Fish and Wildlife
Department of Industry and Natural Resources
Charlottetown, Prince Edward Island, Canada

Quebec:
Director of Wildlife Division
Department of Tourism, Game and Fish
Quebec, Canada

Saskatchewan:
Director of Wildlife
Department of Natural Resources
Government Administration Building
Regina, Saskatchewan, Canada

Yukon Territory:
Game Department, Yukon Territory
White Horse, Yukon Territory, Canada

Also available are government publications, partial lists of which are given below. Farmer's Bulletins and Leaflets are available from the Office of Information, U.S. Department of Agriculture, Washington, D.C. 20250. When you order, give the title, number, and category—Farmer's Bulletin or Leaflet. If you have no response, a letter to your congressman should quickly obtain the publications for you. Give your congressman the numbers and category also.

Farmer's Bulletins:
1055. Hides: Skins, curing and marketing
1334. Home tanning of leather and small skins
1377. Marketing poultry
1378. Marketing eggs
1506. Standard breeds and variations of chickens
1508. Poultry keeping in back yards
1524. Farm poultry raising
1538. Incubation and brooding of chickens
1554. Poultry houses and fixtures
1879. Ponds for wildlife
1938. Fish for food from farm ponds
1983. Farm fish ponds for food and good land use

Leaflets:
233. Selecting breeding stock for broiler production
250. Hamster raising
253. Raising laboratory mice and rats
IS14. If you're thinking of a little place in the country

The Superintendent of Documents, Government Printing Office, Washington, D.C. 20250, sells publications on various subjects, usually for 10 cents for each pamphlet. Order by number and name, and a money order must accompany the order:

10CB. Bobwhite quail propagation
13CB. Feeding wildlife in winter
14CB. Homes for birds
35CB. Fish stocking

From the Fish and Wildlife Service, Department of the Interior, Washington, D.C. 20250, you may obtain publications free by writing for them, ordering by number and name as before:

246WL. Save game meat—it is valuable
17FL. Construction of farm ponds
23FL. Earthworms for bait
27FL. Farm ponds and their management
28FL. Baits
43FL. Care of aquarium fishes
46FL. Dealers in trout and pond fishes
59FL. Construction of a garden fish pool
65FL. Outlet gate for farm fish ponds
97FL. Fish Culture as a livelihood
128FL. Refrigerated locker storage of fish for home use
180FL. Home canning of fish

For rabbit raisers, there is a monthly magazine called *Rabbit World,* published at P.O. Box 107, Marshall, Wisconsin 53559. This publication has a good circulation, and is filled with articles dealing with rabbit culture, nutrition, breeding, genetics, housing and marketing.

Index

susceptibility to diseases of
domestic fowl, 138, 143
raising from eggs, 138-39
state regulations regarding,
138
hatching techniques, 139-40
candling eggs of, 139-40
incubation periods of, 140
brooders for, 138, 140-41
houses and outdoor runs for,
141, 145
danger from owls, 141-42
water supply for, 142
feeding requirements for, 143
controlling parasites and
diseases of, 146
protection from predators, 147-
148
gerbils (Meriones unguicucatus),
111
fallacious theories on, 103-4
breeding, 104, 105
feeding, 104-5
cages for, 105
purposes of raising, 105
temperature for, 105
gram scale, 24
grasshoppers
danger of overcrowding, 50
housing for, 50, 52
feeding, 50-51
breeding, 51-52
importance of warm temperatures and ventilation to, 52
green water, creating, 88-89
See also algae
grouse, 145
incubation period of eggs, 140
ruffed, 145
guinea pigs
for laboratories and schools,
14
cages for, 109-112
long-haired, 110-11
necessity of vitamin C to, 111,
113
breeding, 111, 112
avoiding inbreeding in, 112
floor covering in cages for, 113
feeding, 113

temperature and humidity
requirements for, 113

hamsters, 116
market for, 14, 106
cages for, 106, 109
breeding, 106, 108-9
cannibalism among, 107-8
danger of sunlight to, 107
feeding, 107-8
sensitivity to noises in, 109
sex identification of, 109
hellgrammites
trapping, 70-72
establishing in breeding
stream, 73
mating cage for, 73-74
feeding, 74-75
Himalayan rabbit, 116
hydras, 27-28
feeding habits, 29, 31
collecting wild, 30
for laboratories and schools,
31
reproduction in, 28, 31-32

incubators, mechanical, hatching
game bird eggs in, 138,
139-41
instars (molts) of caterpillars,
66, 67, 68, 69
Io moth, 62

live-trapping of predators, 148

manure for bacterial growth in
ponds, 93
marketing practices with small
animals, 10-11, 12, 13-17,
25, 54, 57, 69, 76, 84-85, 89,
96, 102, 108, 118, 119, 120,
124-125, 137
mealworms, 85
feeding, 53-54, 56
containers for, 53
danger of dampness to, 54
sources and cost of, 54
life cycle of, 54-55
market for, 53, 54
mice, white (Mus musculus)